Going the distance:
How to build your faith for the long haul

Duffy Robbins

A DIVISION OF CTi
CampusLife
BOOKS

ZondervanPublishingHouse
Grand Rapids, Michigan
A Division of HarperCollins*Publishers*

Copyright © 1991 by Youth Specialties, Inc.

Youth Specialties Books, 1224 Greenfield Drive, El Cajon,
    California 92021, are published by Zondervan Publishing House,
    1415 Lake Drive, S.E., Grand Rapids, Michigan 49506

Library of Congress Cataloging-in-Publication Data

Robbins, Duffy.
    Going the distance : how to build a faith for the long haul /
    Duffy Robbins.
        p.   cm.
    ISBN 0-310-54051-8
        1. Church youth workers—Prayer-books and devotions—English.
I. Title.
BV4596.Y68R63 1991
242'.692—dc20

91-6544

CIP

All Scripture quotations, unless otherwise noted, are taken from the *Holy Bible: New International Version* (North American Edition). Copyright © 1973, 1978, 1984 by the International Bible Society. Used by permission of Zondervan Bible Publishers.

Edited by Margery Squier and Kathi George
Design and Typography by JamisonBell Advertising & Design

Printed in the United States of America

91 92 93 94 95 / CH / 10 9 8 7 6 5 4 3 2 1

YOUTHSOURCE™ BOOKS, tapes, videos, and other resources pool the expertise of three of the finest youth ministry resource providers in the world:

- **Campus Life Books**—publishers of the award-winning *Campus Life* magazine, who for nearly fifty years have helped high schoolers live Christian lives.

- **Youth Specialties**—serving ministers to middle school, junior high, and high school youth for over twenty years through books, magazines, and training events such as the National Youth Workers Convention.

- **Zondervan Publishing House**—one of the oldest, largest, and most respected evangelical Christian publishers in the world.

Campus Life	**Youth Specialties**	**Zondervan**
465 Gundersen Dr.	1224 Greenfield Dr.	1415 Lake Dr. S.E.
Carol Stream,	El Cajon,	Grand Rapids,
IL 60188	CA 92021	MI 49506
708/260-6200	619/440-2333	616/698-6900

THIS BOOK IS DEDICATED to my students in the youth ministry program at Eastern College. These people inspire me with their zeal for Christ and excite me with their commitment to youth ministry. Not only have they allowed me to train them and disciple them, they have also allowed me to become their friend. The opportunity to build faith into their lives is a genuine, God-given privilege for which I am extremely grateful. With this book goes the prayer that we will all continue to "press on toward the goal of the upward call of God in Christ Jesus."

Table of Contents

Foreword by Ken Davis.. ix

Chapter   **1**   Preparing for the Race 1

Chapter   **2**   Beware of the Dog(s):
Overcoming Discouragements 15

Chapter   **3**   Running to Win 25

Chapter   **4**   Chalk Talk with the Coach:
Spending Time with God...31

Chapter   **5**   Keeping Pace When the Going Gets Rough 49

Chapter   **6**   Watching Your Tongue:
Inviting Jesus Into Your Mouth 67

Chapter   **7**   Outrunning Temptation:
Taking on the Devil's Triangle 81

Chapter   **8**   The Home Stretch:
Relating to Your Parents..97

Chapter   **9**   Mapping the Course:
Making Wise Decisions...109

Chapter 10   Breaking the Tape...125

VERY FEW BOOKS MAKE ME LAUGH. This one made me laugh out loud. Duffy's rich sense of humor saturates the practical truths presented throughout the book.

The first time I met Duffy Robbins, I thought he needed to be put away. Not completely put out of his misery, you understand, but just put away in a safe place where he couldn't hurt anybody. I love people like Duffy. In fact, if they ever do put him in a padded room, I wouldn't mind being his roommate. Underneath that crazy love for life is a very intelligent and sensitive person who loves teenagers. I have seen him hold teenagers and adults spellbound with his humor and insight. That's just what this book does.

As a teenager, I used to feel stupid trying to be consistent in my life. I ran the race of life in short sprints and spent much of the time sitting on the sidelines. Through much trial and error, and pain and sadness, I was able to get up and continue the race. Fortunately, I will go the distance. I just wish that this book had been available at that time; it has information that can save you much of the grief I had to go through.

Every year I see teenagers lose heart and go off in directions that, at best, derail them from the right path and, at worst, destroy their lives. Some devastate their bodies with alcohol or drugs; some degrade their self-worth by compromising their moral values; some turn their backs on God; others take their own lives. All these kids started the race together, but for some of them, depression, peer pressure, or just the pressures of teenage living distracted them and kept them from going the distance. If they just could have enjoyed this book, then, as they laughed, they would have received the hope that would have allowed them to finish the race. The information you need to go the distance, to live life with the gusto that God meant for it to be lived, is in this book.

After reading *Going the Distance*, I really do believe Duffy needs to be put away. *For safe keeping.* Generations to come should be able to take advantage of Duffy's wisdom and laugh while they are doing it, too!

Ken Davis

Chapter 1:
Preparing for the race

A T FIRST GLANCE, it's easy for people to be fooled by my 5' 5", 185-pound frame, but I am *not* a long distance runner! In fact, I'm not even a short distance runner. I realize it's not very "nineties" of me, and I know that I'm supposed to be jealous of guys jogging along the road wearing multi-colored tights when I pass them going to work on frosty winter mornings. But, honestly, my more realistic gut notion is to sort of swerve in their direction so that they have an opportunity to both run *and* jump! That way they can get some real exercise!

It's not that I'm against distance running. In fact, I enjoy watching it on TV. It's just that driving is faster. When I go out on cold mornings, the only thing that runs on my body is my nose.

And yet, as I sit here at my desk working on this book, there is a sense in which I am a distance runner. There is a sense in which I am totally and completely absorbed in running a marathon. You see, over twenty years ago, on a Thanksgiving Young Life weekend at a small camp near Greenville, South Carolina, for the first time in my life, I prayed a simple prayer giving my-self to Jesus Christ. It was the first step in a long walk.

Since that amazing night, there have been a lot of steps forward and a lot of steps back. There have been other times when I seemed to stop dead in my tracks. There have even been some times when I almost wandered away from the race altogether. But, by the grace and forgiveness of an incredibly loving God, it's been over twenty years now, and I'm still pressing on.

Going the distance with Jesus

O NE OF THE MOST IMPORTANT LESSONS of the Christian life is that God isn't so much into speed as he is into distance. The Christian life is not a sprint. It's a marathon—not a halfhearted commitment that wilts when the heat's on, or fades into the background when it's mixed in with the crowd. God has called us to go the distance—a consistent step-by-step, forward motion that continues over the long haul. That's really what it means to "remain in him" or "abide in him" (John 15). It's a commitment to go the distance with Jesus.

The thing is, our desire to go the distance with Jesus can be hard to apply in real life. Many times, I've had students come up to me after I've spoken about building a long-haul faith and say something like, "Duffy, I really *want* to have a faith that lasts. But *how* can I make that work in my everyday life—at school, with my friends, with my family, and even with my bratty little brother?"

That's why I've written this book. I believe God has given us some practical steps we can follow that will help us make our faith work in real life. In the following chapters, we'll look at those steps, and we'll see how they can have an impact on the tough areas of our lives, like dealing with depression, relating to our parents, coping with pressure from our friends, learning to spend time with God, and more. It's not always easy, but it's exciting—and the results are worth it.

Tips for the long haul

O NE THING I LOVE ABOUT THE BIBLE is that it's so
practical. Through writers like the apostle Paul,
God has given us examples we can identify with and
make sense of in everyday life. There's a passage from
Paul's letter to the Philippians that I'd like us to focus
on as we consider building a
long-haul faith.

In the third chapter of
Philippians, Paul gives some
good advice for those of us
who want to go the distance
with Jesus. Nobody said it
was going to be easy, but
Paul's words are practical
and they ring with the echo
of experience.

*God isn't so
much into speed
as he is into
distance. The
Christian life is
not a sprint;
it's a marathon.*

Finally, my brothers, re-
joice in the Lord! It is no
trouble for me to write
the same things to you again,
and it is a safeguard for you.

Watch out for those dogs,
those men who do evil, those mu-
tilators of the flesh. For it is
we who are the circumci-
sion [AUTHOR'S NOTE: If
you don't understand what circumcision is, see the diagram on page 4],
we who worship by the Spirit of
God, who glory in Christ Jesus,
and who put no confidence in
the flesh—though I myself have
reasons for such confidence.

If anyone else thinks he has reasons

We were only kidding about that circumcision diagram; didn't mean to scare you. Seriously, if you don't know what circumcision is, try this: Go to your telephone right now, call your pastor, and ask him. This is a great way to start a conversation with your pastor and a fun way to meet people on your church staff. For extra credit: Have your sister make the call. For extra, extra credit: Have your mom make the call. For extra, extra, extra credit: Draw a diagram based on your conversation with the pastor and share it in Sunday school next week.

to put confidence in the flesh, I have more: circumcised on the eighth day, of the people of Israel, of the
tribe of Benjamin, a Hebrew of Hebrews; in regard
to the law, a Pharisee; as for zeal, persecuting the
church; as for legalistic righteousness, faultless.

But whatever was to my profit I now consider
loss for the sake of Christ. What is more, I consider
everything a loss compared to the surpassing greatness of knowing Christ Jesus my Lord, for whose
sake I have lost all things. I consider them rubbish,
that I may gain Christ and be found in him, not having a righteousness of my own that comes from the
law, but that which is through faith in Christ—the
righteousness that comes from God and is by faith. I
want to know Christ and the power of his resurrection and the fellowship of sharing in his sufferings,
becoming like him in his death, and so, somehow, to
attain to the resurrection from the dead.

Not that I have already obtained all this, or
have already been made perfect, but I press on to
take hold of that for which Christ Jesus took hold of
me. Brothers, I do not consider myself yet to have
taken hold of it. But one thing I do: Forgetting what
is behind and straining toward what is ahead, I press
on toward the goal to win the prize for which God
has called me heavenward in Christ Jesus.
Philippians 3:1-14

If we were to sum up this passage, what Paul tells
us about going the distance with Jesus Christ would
boil down to three basic ideas: Be prepared to face opposition, keep a single-minded focus on your goal, and
run to win. We'll be covering all of Paul's points in later
chapters; right now, let's focus on his call to single-
mindedness.

Be single-minded

ONE OF MY ALL-TIME FAVORITE MOVIES is *Chariots of Fire*, the story of Scottish marathon runner Eric Liddell and his quest for gold in the 1933 Olympic games. How could you watch the opening scene of those men running down the beach in their boxers in the early dawn—the slow-motion footage capturing every grimace, every strain, every neck muscle—without being awed by their stamina? It's incredible. Every time I watch the thing, I want to go stand in front of the mirror and practice running in slow motion. (In fact, I scared my daughter the other day. She came home after school, went down the hall, turned the corner—and there I was in my boxers, running in slow motion toward the bathroom mirror.)

If we want to go the distance in the Christian life, we can't look back. We have to look forward and press on.

One of the reasons those opening shots are so amazing is that the slow motion camera allows us to see the intensity of these men—every muscle, every sinew, every fiber dedicated to one, and only one, goal: the finish line. We can see it in their eyes. We can see it in their legs. These guys have one thing on their minds. It's inconceivable that Eric Liddell would slow his pace, veer from the track, and say, "H - e - y, l - o - o - k !

T-h-e-r-e'-s a p-r-e-t-t-y s-h-e-l-l!" No way. This is a picture of single-minded determination.

Paul says that if we want to go the distance in the Christian life, we have to be single-minded in the same way. We can't look back; we can't look off. We've got to look forward and press on. Paul writes:

> ... one thing I do: Forgetting what is behind and straining toward what is ahead, I press on toward the goal to win the prize for which God has called me heavenward in Christ Jesus. *Philippians 3:13-14*

I'll never forget one afternoon before my wife and I were married. We were on a date at a lake house in North Carolina. It was a beautiful sunny afternoon. She was sitting on the porch of the boathouse and I was down below on the dock showing off for her. (This was a pretty normal deal for us. I spent a lot of time showing off, and she spent a lot of time acting as if I was funny. You know how it works.)

What I was doing really *was* kind of funny. I was standing with one foot on the dock while the other was perched on the side of the boat, and I was rocking back and forth. To make a long story short, the next thing I knew, I saw a guy doing this incredible spread eagle ... and realized it was *me*.

It was obvious that either I had to take immediate action or I was headed for "mega-baptism." Fortunately, it was a two-tiered dock—the upper tier about six feet above the water, and the lower tier on which I was standing, about eighteen inches above the water. With a little luck, it looked like I just might be able to lunge for the corner pole of that upper dock and save myself the embarrassment of an unplanned swim. In my mind's eye, I could see myself soaring like an eagle and coming to a graceful roost, high and dry on the corner post. . . . As you might imagine, a situation like that doesn't allow a lot of time for thought and strategy. There was nothing to do but jump, and jump is exactly what I did. . . .

The good news is that I hit the dock. The bad news is *where* I hit the dock. I guess, with hindsight, flying into the corner pillar of the dock with my legs spread apart was probably not a wise thing to do. My first move, upon making contact with the dock, was to double over. The eagle was, indeed, sore!

I learned a lesson that day, and it's right at the heart of the basic spiritual truth Paul teaches in this passage: Indecision causes pain.

Splish splash

S O MANY TIMES we try to live our Christian lives by putting one foot on the world's dock and one foot in God's boat, and we just keep getting spread out farther and farther until the compromise and indecision eventually lead us to some major pain. That's why Paul's basic instruction for going the distance with Jesus is that we must be single-minded.

That's not very easy in the world most of us live in today. Our parents want us to go one way, school wants us to go another way, the church wants us to go still another, and our friends are pulling us in a fourth direction. The temptation is to try to please everybody. We firmly plant one foot on the world's dock, not wanting to go against the crowd, or not wanting to end a relationship, or not being willing to give up a dream. But, at the same time, we place the other foot in God's boat and begin to realize that he is pulling us away from these old securities and priorities. It becomes a treacherous stretch. It may have to do with the group of friends we hang around with, the way we spend our money, the way we use our mouth, or the kinds of music and movies we enjoy. It might have to do with goals we choose for our life. It may just have to do with the way we see ourselves and how we want others to see us. Sooner or later, we're usually brought to that position when we have to make a clear, single-minded choice: Where will we stand? On the world's dock, or in God's boat? There is no middle ground, and the prolonged indecision causes pain. For Paul it came down to a single-minded commitment to Christ: this ". . . one thing I do."

Don't look back

O F COURSE, ONE REASON IT'S SO TOUGH sometimes to be single-minded about the race ahead of us is that we often drag emotional baggage along with us. Some of you who are reading this book are having a tough time moving forward because of some very painful stuff in your past. That's why Paul says that single-mindedness can only happen when we begin by ". . . Forgetting what is behind. . . ."

Obviously, Paul is not suggesting here that we act like the painful stuff didn't happen, or that the pain isn't still real. We need to bury the past. That's true. But we'd better not bury it alive. It may be that the first step you will have to take to really become focused and single-minded in your walk with Jesus is to seek counseling about your past. Sometimes we need that kind of help to forget what lies behind.

For others of us, the wounds are self-inflicted. Bad decisions, wrong choices, or ghosts of guilt haunt our past and hold down our pace as we try to press on with Christ. Perhaps, we need to begin by just honestly going to God and admitting that we've sinned—that we've gotten off the track and tried to go our own way. It may even be that we owe some people some apologies, and we will need to seek them out and ask their forgiveness. The great miracle of God's love is that if we confess our sins, God is willing to forgive us and clear away the guilt and pain of earlier indecision.

We won't run very far in our Christian lives if we drag along a load of hurts, painful memories, and unconfessed sin. We need to deal with the past, and that's not always very pleasant. That's why some people go through their whole lives blaming their past for their present and their future. "If only my parents had done this. . . ." "If the teacher hadn't done that. . . ." "If only I didn't. . . ." It's almost easier sometimes to cop out on the future than it is to cope with our past. In the end, the choice is ours to make. But if we hope to run the race with any genuine single-mindedness, we've got to forget what lies behind.

Getting off our "but's"

A NYONE WHO HAS EVER GONE THROUGH the agony of learning to ski will recall that everybody is eager to give advice to the beginning skier. People have some really helpful insights. They say things like: "Ski in control at all times," even though common sense tells you that this will only be possible if you ski without your skis on. Or they start you off with confidence builders like: "Let's learn how to fall correctly." And, of course, you're thinking, "Boy, *this* sounds like lots of fun!"

I do remember, however, hearing one basic principle of downhill skiing that has stayed with me. A high school guy I was skiing with advised me to always keep my weight out over the tips of the skis. He said, "It won't feel natural to you to lean forward that way (he was right), but it will keep you from falling as much (he was wrong)." It seemed so strange to lean out over the tips of the skis when my natural instinct was to sit back on the rear of the skis. It made more sense to me to let the tips of the skis kind of go down the hill ahead of me, and if they made it all right, I would follow them. Unfortunately, as I demonstrated to the many people standing and laughing in the lift line, this "weight back—play it safe" approach is the procedure for creating a human snowball.

And the same basic principle is at work in the Christian life. According to Paul, single-mindedness in the spiritual life is not just a matter of "forgetting what is behind," it is also the discipline of "straining toward what is ahead" (Philippians 3:13). It's really a willingness to say, "Okay, Lord, I'm not sure what's going to happen if I obey you in this, or if I take this step of faith, but let's go for it."

One of the toughest parts to being single-minded with Christ is that most of us want to play it safe.

You see, one of the toughest parts of being single-minded in a walk with Christ is that most of us tend to want to play it safe. We want to be a Christian in our schools and in our families and in our relationships and among our friends, but sometimes that can be kind of scary.

We don't always know where obedience is going to lead us. We don't have any guarantees about where we're going to land. So, we tend to respond, "Okay, Lord, I'll obey you, but . . ." or "I'll do everything you've asked, but. . . ." And, of course, what happens is we end up falling on our "but's." That's why Paul says the bottom line (no pun intended) for staying balanced in the Christian life is to strain forward and go for broke, "no if's, and's, or but's."

Finish or bust!

SOME TIME AGO, I read a magazine article recounting the results of a recent Boston Marathon, the twenty-six-mile race that stretches from suburban Hopkinton to downtown Boston. The article reported the winner as Alberto Salazar, perennial marathon champion, who finished the race in the record-breaking time of two hours, eight minutes, and fifty one seconds. But the article went on to observe that Salazar's finish was no more remarkable than the extraordinary finish of thirty-eight-year old Guy Gertsch.

Gertsch, a Salt Lake City bus station ticket agent, finished the race in the rather ordinary time of two hours and forty-seven minutes. What was amazing was that he did it with a broken leg. In post-race interviews, Gertsch said he felt what he thought was a cramp starting around the seven-mile mark. But he was determined to finish the race, so he pounded the pavement for nineteen more miles before finally collapsing at the finish line. Doctors, who later set his right femur with a steel rod, could only guess that the powerful muscles in his right thigh had acted as a natural splint to hold the broken bone in place until he finally relaxed it at the race's end.

The fact of the matter is that some of you reading this book are even today writing your own amazing story of determination. God has called you to move forward in obedience to him—not just to begin this race, but to finish it; not just to meet Christ, but to "remain in him." It's a long haul. The route is tough. Many of you have even faced some pretty bad breaks. But, you're determined to finish. All of us need to consistently ask ourselves if our commitment to Christ is characterized by a genuine single-mindedness. We need to ask ourselves if we are willing to turn from the world's dock and plant both feet firmly in God's boat. Some of us will only be able to take the step forward when we have first stepped back to deal with our past. It can be painful, but we need to take inventory to make sure that we can bury our past without burying it alive.

Still others of us need to be honest enough to admit that our single-mindedness is blurred by a desire to "play it safe." Maybe we need to take a moment right now to think of specific areas where God is calling us to get up off our "but's" and take some risks for him.

There's no question that all of this can be pretty intimidating. But don't forget that Jesus is not waiting for you somewhere at the end of the race; he is running the race with you. He is there to guide you as you run, and he's there to help you up when you fall. He is the one who helps you to go the distance:

> Therefore . . . let us throw off everything that hinders and the sin that so easily entangles, and let us run with perseverance the race marked out for us. Let us fix our eyes on Jesus, the author and perfecter of our faith. . . . *Hebrews 12:1, 2*

Chapter 2:
Beware of the dog(s): Overcoming discouragements

One of my least favorite memories as a teenager is my one-year hitch as a paper boy. For one thing, I had to get up at about four in the morning. For another thing . . . well, frankly, there didn't need to be another thing because that was more than enough reason for me to hate the job. But, to add insult to injury, I had to begin this "midnight ride" every morning by biking through a jungle of big, pesky dogs. Believe me, there is nothing worse than pedaling along your route with your eyes closed, trying to stay asleep and deliver newspapers at the same time—sort of coasting on automatic pilot—when all of a sudden, out of the morning mist, comes Fido the Thirteenth barking and howling and showing his teeth.

Of course, everyone has advice for you when you are being approached by a barking dog. Some say you should, "Just freeze." Well, I'm sorry, but that sounds plain stupid to me. I can almost see it in this dog's eyes. He's thinking, "Oh boy, frozen food! Look, everybody . . . Swanson's!!"

Then there are those who flash that knowing smile and respond, "Hey, the key is not to let the dog know you're scared. If the dog sees that you're scared, he'll become aggressive." Okay, I understand that. But when there is a huge dog snarling at my foot, and blood is running down my leg, the truth is, I *am* scared. I admit it.

Others say, "If a dog is chasing you, just run. Get out of there." All right, I like the sound of that, but when I used to try that on my bike, it only seemed to inspire these dogs. It almost seemed that they were thinking, "Gosh, what a great workout. This is fun!"

And, finally, there are those—and these are the people who just frost me—who watch from the porch as their dog chases you down the street, and just as their dog starts to literally hijack your bike, yell, "Don't worry, he won't bite!" Oh yeah? I felt like yelling back, "*You* know he doesn't bite, and *I* know he doesn't bite, but does *he* know he doesn't bite?"

When times are "Ruff"

I suppose that distance runners must hate dogs as much as paper boys do. Dogs bark at you. They chase you. They distract you. They make a tough run even tougher. And yet, in an entire year of delivering newspapers every morning, I never once confronted a dog who jumped out in front of me with his paws raised yelling, "Halt!" or "Hey you, pull over." Dogs can't do that. They can slow you down. And they can make you veer off course. But they cannot stop you.

I think that's why Paul begins his instruction in Philippians 3 by reminding fellow runners to "watch out for those dogs":

> Watch out for those dogs, those men who do evil, those mutilators of the flesh. . . . *Philippians 3:2*

Now admittedly, this is not one of those verses you hear quoted very often in Vacation Bible School. I can't ever recall seeing it done on a flannelgraph. In fact, I guess I always just figured that dogs weren't even invented until sometime back in the 1600s or something. But, for Paul the apostle, there were some very real dogs nipping at his heels. They didn't actually bark or bite, but they made a lot of noise, and they were constantly chasing after Paul and the other disciples.

Distractions can't stop us, but they can slow us down or push us in the wrong direction.

Their charge was that Paul was a hoax, that this Christianity business was a sham, and that Jesus was an outlaw, a nut, or both, who had messed up everybody's mind with his teaching about the love and grace of God. Essentially, they charged that Paul was preaching a phony gospel, and that people could only come to God by obeying the man-made legalism of the temple. And although they could never stop Paul's work for Christ, there were several occasions when their opposition threatened to slow him down or force him to veer off course.

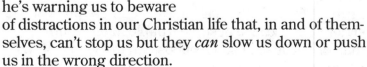

When Paul warns us to "watch out for the dogs," he's warning us to beware of distractions in our Christian life that, in and of themselves, can't stop us but they *can* slow us down or push us in the wrong direction.

Most of us know exactly what Paul is talking

about. There are people in our lives who seem to make it real hard to go the distance with Jesus. We're trying to walk with Christ on a daily basis, moving along all right, and then we confront these people who start nipping at our heels. Sometimes it's a parent. Other times it's a friend. It might be a teacher at school, or even a member of the congregation at church. Sometimes the barks are even self-inflicted. Most of the time, the bark is worse than the bite, but that doesn't make it any easier to press on.

The dog show

WHAT ARE SOME OF THE "DOGS" we face? Well, there are a variety of different species that seem to chase after student disciples. Below is a list to help you identify some of them so that you can be on your guard.

Terrier. These are the people who are always wringing their hands, terrified about how bad everything is. To hear them talk, God has more or less gone behind a cloud for a while, and now, in the meantime, the sky is falling! Whether they are talking about something as local as the youth group or as cosmic as the environment, these people are able to see all the reasons why we can't succeed, and why we can't move forward any farther. These people are always up for a good panic.

You usually hear the Terriers start howling when the school administration cracks down on a campus prayer meeting, or when it won't let the youth group distribute flyers in the hallway. Sometimes you hear the Terrier yelp because of some trouble in the youth group or because of some opposition to the ministry. At first glance, there appears to be every reason to give up and run scared.

The problem is that the Terriers have forgotten how big God is. No one ever said that living the Christian life was going to be easy. No one ever said that we wouldn't face opposition. What we tend to forget is that we already know how the story's going to end, and the good guys always come out on top.

Paul faced all kinds of opposition in his ministry, and all kinds of accusations from people trying to slow him down and discredit his work. But Paul believed in a God who is in control. He didn't just sit around whining, "Oh no . . . look what the world has come to." He just kept pushing forward, preaching, "Look who has come to the world!" If we try to do something for Jesus on our campus, or in our church, or among our friends, we're likely to face some tough going. But, we need to remember that a sovereign God is in control. We may need to be creative. We may need to be resourceful. And we may have to go through some scary stuff to keep moving forward, but God will make a way for us. We have to watch out that the Terriers don't scare us off course.

Pointer. These are the people who always seem to make you feel that you aren't spiritual enough. You know the type. "You can't be a real Christian because you're not wearing a coat and tie to church." "You must not be very spiritual because you're not serious enough." "That can't be Christian music. Listen to it . . . it's rock and roll." "Real Christians don't struggle with those kinds of things." The Pointer is always there to point the finger and growl every time you lose your balance or fall.

What is strange about the Pointer is that when we finally meet one face to face, it's us! Many times we get so down on ourselves that we're our own worst enemies. What usually happens is that we're trucking along, going the distance with Jesus, when one way or another we trip, we sin, we fall. And then, while we're down, a little voice from inside tells us, "You can't be serious calling yourself a Christian. You're about as authentic as Milli Vanilli. Real Christians don't have these kinds of problems. Real Christians don't struggle with these kinds of temptations. Don't you dare ask for forgiveness. You're not serious about walking with Jesus!"

> *The way to deal with guilt is to confess it to the Lord, get back on our feet, and start walking again.*

And of course, what happens is that this unconfessed sin messes up our fellowship with God. It doesn't end our relationship with God, it just clouds our fellowship. The problem is that when we're limping along out of fellowship with God, we're even more likely to fall again the next time, and the whole cycle just repeats itself.

I love the story about the high school guy who walked into his youth minister's office because he was superfrustrated. He wanted to be a godly guy and everything, but he was struggling with lust—big time. As he sat there in his youth worker's office, he just got more and more frustrated and more and more discouraged. "Doggone it, I'm sorry, I'm trying to be a good Christian, and I don't want to lust, but, man, I see these great-looking girls in the hallway and you wouldn't believe the stuff that goes through my mind!"

This guy just kept getting madder and madder, pounding on his youth worker's desk, until finally he screamed, "I've had it! I'm praying right now: Lord take away my sexual desire. . . . " Immediately, his youth worker yells, "Wait a minute!! Let me leave the room in case God misses!"

Discouragement is a big stumbling block for students who want to go the distance with Christ. Watch out for the Pointer. It's true that sometimes the Holy Spirit convicts us of wrongdoing, and the reason we feel guilty is because we *are* guilty! But the way to deal with guilt is to confess it to the Lord, get back on our feet, and start walking again. Jesus said, "For God did not send his Son into the world to condemn the world, but to save the world through him" (John 3:17).

Boxer. The Boxers are those people in our lives who know exactly what God can do and what God can't do. They've got God all figured out so that he fits in their little box. People who put God in a box always tell you that he can't be trusted for this, or that he isn't big enough to do that.

Obviously, they can't stop God from being God, but they can rationalize us off the course of faith. "You gotta be kidding; you're going to witness to that guy? He'll never become a Christian." "It won't do any good to pray for your folks' marriage. God doesn't work like that." "You can't really believe that God is going to heal your friend. That kind of stuff doesn't happen in this modern age." The Boxer can fool us into thinking that we "better not try this," or we "better not pray for that; we better play it safe." In short, we better not count on God actually being God.

Bulldog. These people have an especially intimidating bark because they sound so intelligent. The Bulldog usually hangs out in classrooms telling people that the Christian faith simply is not intellectually credible—that you have to be brain dead to really believe the Bible. In short, what they are spreading is 100 percent *bull!*

Any honest study of history and archaeology will turn up ample evidence that demonstrates that the Bible is a book that can be trusted. That doesn't mean that Christian scholars have an answer for every question, or that there aren't areas of confusion. But judging the Bible solely on the basis of human intellect is like trying to find the sun with a flashlight.

It takes faith to believe in God. That's true. We cannot prove he exists. On the other hand, it also takes faith not to believe in God, because no one can prove that he doesn't exist. Either way it's a posture of faith.

I once heard a story about a high school girl sitting in her religious studies class. Shelley was only a sophomore, but as a Christian she was getting a little tired of her pompous teacher making fun of Christians and leading everyone to believe that Christians were a bunch of airheads.

So one day, as the teacher was barking out his lines, he made this statement: "Christianity cannot be true, because there is no such thing as absolute truth." Quietly, Shelley raised her hand, and asked in a steady voice, "Is that absolutely true?" And of course, he assured her that it was. At which point she responded, "Then you must be wrong." Hmmmm . . . nice dog . . . heel, boy.

Their bark is worse than their bite

WHATEVER DOGS are coming after you, the important strategy is not to get intimidated. Keep on with the race! Remember: Jesus is really "man's best friend." When you hear that barking in your ears, just turn around, look that dog in the face, and say, "In the name of Jesus, *be heeled!*"

Chapter 3:
Running to win

HAVE YOU EVER NOTICED what happens every year when the yearbooks are passed out at school? People start to play this little game in which the contestants start reading all of the activities under their senior pictures to see who has the longest list of stuff. It's great! People who are really good at it can sneak in something like "French Club" or "Dead Poets' Society" or "Society for the Preservation of Homo sapiens" without anybody ever realizing it's a bluff. And, of course, you get bonus points for things like "Most Likely to Succeed," "Most Likely to Be Most Likable," or "Most Likely to Commit A Felony."

I didn't realize it when I was in high school, but that game is actually great preparation for real life. You see, it wasn't until I graduated from college that I began to realize how many of us spend our entire lifetimes adding up titles and honors and memberships that don't really mean much, but that make us look like winners in the eyes of the world.

The apostle Paul knew that game well. In fact, at one time in his life he was All-Pro. He had every duck lined up, every base covered, and every honor given. He was a first-class stud. In Philippians 3:3-11, Paul reminds us that if stacking up honors is the game, he can play it with the best of them: ". . . we who worship by the Spirit of God, who glory in Christ Jesus . . . put no confidence in the flesh—though I myself have reasons for such confidence.

"If anyone else thinks he has reasons to put confidence in the flesh, I have more: circumcised on the eighth day. . . ."

(Now there's something you don't hear a lot of guys bragging about. Can you imagine under your senior picture: Soccer: 2, 3, 4; Honor Society: 2, 3, 4; Circumcised: 8th day!? Impressive!)

". . . of the people of Israel, of the tribe of Benjamin, a Hebrew of Hebrews; in regard to the law, a Pharisee; as for zeal, persecuting the church; as for legalistic righteousness, faultless."

Basically, Paul is saying, "Look, if you want to talk resumes, I've got it. You name the title, I've got the plaque." But, he says, that's not the whole story. He goes on to make an incredibly radical statement: ". . . whatever was to my profit I now consider loss for the sake of Christ. What is more, I consider everything a loss compared to the surpassing greatness of knowing Christ Jesus my Lord, for whose sake I have lost all things. I consider them rubbish, that I may gain Christ and be found in him, not having a righteousness of my own that comes from the law, but that which is through faith in Christ—the righteousness that comes from God and is by faith. I want to know Christ and the power of his resurrection and the fellowship of sharing in his sufferings, becoming like him in his death, and so, somehow, to attain to the resurrection from the dead."

Going for the win

EVERYWHERE WE TURN NOWADAYS, people encourage us to "go for it." Teachers want us to "go for good grades." Society says, "Go for the big bucks." Friends say, "Go for popularity." Spuds says, "Go for the party." It's not easy to figure out what the "it" is we're supposed to be going for.

If we hope to go the distance in the Christian life, Paul tells us that we can't afford to get distracted by all the goodies, titles, and honors that are supposed to make us winners in the eyes of the world. Paul writes that there was a time when he had put all of his "confidence in the flesh," and all of his hopes were staked on his own talents, abilities, and dreams. But God opened his eyes to see that it was all nothing but "rubbish," literally "dung," "compared to the surpassing greatness of knowing Christ Jesus. . . ."

We can't afford to be distracted by the honors that make us look like winners in the eyes of the world.

Does that mean that you shouldn't be involved in sports or in band? Does that mean that schoolwork is unimportant, or that a college degree is a waste of time? Not at all. It's not that there is anything bad about excelling in sports or in academics or in any other field. In fact, we need to try to do our very best in whatever we do, to the glory of God. The Bible tells us it's a sin to waste our God-given abilities. (See the book of Matthew, chapter 25, verses 14-30, if you don't believe me.)

The danger is that we often focus too much on all of these things. We lose our perspective and forget our goal. We want to run for the good job or the nice car or the big house or the prestigious title. And although we may end up a winner in the eyes of the world, that may very well make us a loser in the kingdom of God.

Not long ago, I read an article in *Sports Illustrated* profiling various professional athletes who excel in their sports year after year, season after season. Unlike the typical athlete who shoots up like a rising star for one season, but then sort of sinks to the All-"Twinkie" team the next season, these were consistent performers who had hung in there with excellence over the long haul. I was particularly impressed by a comment in the article from Dave Parker, one of the most respected competitors in baseball. Parker was discussing the telling moment when a ball is hit way back toward the fence and the outfielder begins to backpedal hard until he realizes he's on the warning track near the wall. That, says Parker, is where you can tell those who are in it for the right reasons and those who are in it for the glory: "Some guys won't go into the wall, you know? They've got numbers on their minds. But, I learned a long time ago. . . . You either play for the stats, or you play for the wins."

We have two choices in life. We can play for all those stats that make us winners in the world: money, fame, power, prestige, honor, titles, and so on. Or we can begin to count as garbage anything that gets in the way of our daily relationship with Jesus Christ. Paul coaches us to go for the wins.

Counting the garbage

MAYBE THIS IS A GOOD TIME to ask ourselves: What race are we running? What prize do we seek? What are our motivations? Some of us are urged by well-meaning people—parents, teachers, and counselors—to put the statistics of the world ahead of the prize of the kingdom. We're told, "I hope you're not going to medical school just so you can go to some mission field and work for bananas." Or, "You don't have time to play in all-state band and be in the discipleship group, too. You'd better take the trumpet over the Bible. Colleges don't look at spiritual commitment." Or, "Of course we want you involved in youth group, but you've got to keep up your tennis lessons if you hope to get that important scholarship."

The challenge of the race of faith is to stay focused on the heavenward call of God in Christ Jesus (Philippians 3:14). It takes a single-mindedness that strains forward and stays focused, pushing aside the distractions and moving toward the goal. That will not always be easy, but in the end, we will come to "know Christ and the power of his resurrection" (Philippians 3:10).

If you've tasted the excitement of that race, don't turn back. My prayer for you is that you will continue to press on! Never settle for a few lousy stats when you can go for the wins!

Chapter 4:
Chalk talk with the coach:
Spending time with God

I HAD SPOKEN IN THIS CHURCH several times, so the offer didn't catch me totally off guard. Through previous visits to Mount Oak Church, I had gotten a chance to meet many in the congregation, and I knew a lot of them held rather unique and interesting government jobs. It was not unusual on a Sunday morning to be ushered to your seat by a Pentagon consultant, hear a testimony by an FBI agent, and pass the offering plate to a congressional aide. But Steve Eckersley's job was particularly intriguing. He was in charge of all the Secret Service agents working in the White House.

He came up to me after I had spoken in the Sunday evening service and offered me an invitation. He said he would like to take my wife and me to the White House on Monday morning so that we could meet the president of the United States. Well, obviously we were blown away. We were thinking, "Gosh, what a treat this will be for the president!" So we said, "Great, let's do it!"

Standing there in the back of the church, we worked through all of the logistical plans for the next morning. Steve made it very clear that we should meet him at the West Gate of the White House promptly at 7:30 a.m. so that he could take us on this tour. One of the reasons we had to be in and out so early was because a Cabinet meeting was scheduled for 8:15 and Steve didn't feel they would appreciate us walking through the room during the meeting. He advised us that if we were going to be in center-city Washington by 7:30 Monday morning, we would have to leave the home we were staying at by about 6:30. That meant rise-and-shine no later than 5:30.

Well, that Sunday night we went to bed with our heads spinning. We couldn't believe that we were going to be standing in the Oval Office within eight hours. It took us a while to settle down to sleep, but finally we drifted off.

During what seemed like the middle of the night, I was awakened by the phone ringing. I couldn't figure out who would be calling at that time of night, but I heard footsteps across the floor above us as someone moved to answer the phone. Then, within a few moments, I could see the light from upstairs enter the stairway as Carol, my hostess, yelled downstairs, "Duffy, are you awake? Telephone for you. . . . It's the White House!"

Well, by this time I have to admit I was feeling kind of cocky, so I leaned over to my wife and said, "I hope they're not going to ask us to stick around for that Cabinet meeting. We've got things to do."

I stumbled to the phone, still half asleep, only to be greeted by an urgent voice: "Duffy, is that you? Where are you? Do you know what time it is?" I was still sort of in the Twilight Zone so I asked, "Who is this?"

"It's Steve Eckersley. Duffy, I'm calling from the White House. Do you realize what time it is?"

"Well, no, I . . ."

"Duffy, it's 7:45. I was just calling to make sure you guys were on your way. If you haven't left yet, there's no way you're going to get down here in time. We're going to have to can the whole deal this morning. Look, I'm sorry. Maybe the next time you come to Mount Oak we can set something up."

By the time I hung up the phone, my wife knew something was up. She had only heard my end of the conversation, but she could tell something wasn't right.

When I got back to bed, she asked what the problem was and I knew I had to tell her: "Maggie . . . I don't know how to tell you this . . . but you have got to be married to one of the only guys in the country . . . who has slept through a chance to meet the president of the United States!"

Why do we pass up our chance to meet daily with the King of Kings? We simply don't know what we're missing.

The expression on her face, even through the darkness, said it all. I knew exactly what she was thinking. She was thinking . . . well, she was thinking exactly the same thing you're thinking as you read this story: "What a complete idiot!"

Actually, before I leave this story, I need to make two comments about the episode.

Number one: it never happened. I made it up.

Number two: actually, it did happen. In fact, it happened to me this morning. And it happens every day to thousands of people.

I don't mean that people are sleeping through a chance to go the Oval Office and meet the president of the United States. What I mean is that people just like me and you, on days just like this one, sleep right through a chance to go into the throne room of almighty God and talk to the Creator of the universe. Every new day greets us with a chance to get out of bed and spend a few minutes with God, but most of us just blow it off for a few extra minutes of sleep.

Meeting time

T HE PURPOSE OF THIS CHAPTER is not to make you feel like some guilt-ridden, spiritually impaired sleep monger. Meeting with God on a consistent basis is not some kind of legalistic requirement that you have to meet before God will love you. God is not up in heaven with a roll book and a stopwatch tabulating who really deserves his love. We spend time with God because he does love us, unconditionally, and because we want to further develop and deepen our relationship with him.

I'm also not going to tell you that the discipline of spending time with God on a regular basis is a piece of cake; that after you've been a Christian for a while, it seems only natural and easy to spring from your bed on cold winter mornings and skip to your Bible while the rest of the house is dark. I've been a Christian for a long time, and I've got to be honest, I still don't jump out of the sack, grab my Bible, and sing, "Good morning, Lord!" I'm just like you when I wake up in the morning. I fall out of bed, stumble to the bathroom, and say, "Good Lord, it's morning."

We don't know what we're missing

I THINK I UNDERSTAND WHY we pass up this audience with the King of Kings, why we slumber in our beds when we could be talking to the Creator of the universe. Most of us simply don't realize what we're missing. "Why should I get up early to study a book I'm not even going to be tested on?" "And what's the point of waking up to pray when I could get a few extra minutes of sleep? My eyes will be closed either way, right?"

Actually, there are three good reasons for having what people sometimes call "daily devotions" or a "Quiet Time." To begin with, the heart of the Christian walk is developing a relationship with God through his Son Jesus. There is no way a relationship with anyone can develop if we don't give it time. Try telling your best friend, "I really love you a lot and I really value our relationship; it's just that I don't ever want to talk with you unless I'm in trouble, in need, or report cards are coming out the next day." It's not the best way to nurture a friendship. If we really want to get to know God, we need to spend time with him.

Second, a consistent Quiet Time keeps us on course as we go the distance with Christ. God speaks to us through the Bible and gives us instruction about how we are to run the race.

Life can be pretty confusing. You tend to get pulled in many different directions. People expect you to make all kinds of choices and decisions. It's tough. And it gets even tougher when the culture more or less tells you that there is no such thing as right or wrong. "What's right is what's right for you." After a while, we start to feel like the drunk who said, "All day long I've been asking people what time it is, and all day long I've gotten a different answer."

What's the point of going the distance if we're running in the wrong direction? The Scripture is one of the main ways God gives us guidance. As David put it in Psalm 119:105, "Your word is a lamp to my feet and a light for my path."

Third, consistent devotions are like spiritual maintenance. As a teenager, I was drafted every summer to mow the lawn around our house. It was one of those jobs that I particularly disliked. (The general rule of thumb was that I didn't like any job that actually involved labor—or work of any kind.) But mowing the lawn was a special pain because it had to be done with such regularity. Every week—twice a week in July—I would have to push this loud, heavy (antique) mower through our lawn under a hot summer sun.

Daily devotions play a vital part in our program of consistent spiritual maintenance.

I know people who say they really enjoy mowing the lawn. I am not one of them. Some people say, "It gives me time to think." Right. It gives me time to think, too. It's just that what I'm thinking about is how much I don't enjoy mowing the lawn! And, of course, if I skipped a week my dad would drop little hints like, "You might need to mow the lawn, Son; we lost your sister in the backyard yesterday." Or, "Duffy, would you get your mother a machete? She's trying to bring in the groceries." I'm sorry, I'm just not one of those

36

people who gets high on grass.

I think what especially aggravated me about mowing the lawn was that it wouldn't stay mowed. It could be mowed once on Monday and by Saturday it needed to be mowed again. That's frustrating. A lawn that looks great the first weekend in June will look like a jungle by August if someone doesn't continue to maintain it. Where once there was a beautiful green carpet, there is now an ugly stretch of weeds and thorns.

The same is true in our spiritual lives. If we want to go the distance with Jesus, we need to practice consistent spiritual maintenance. The Christian commitment that looks great one week after summer camp can look like a jungle of sin and misplaced priorities three months later if it hasn't received some maintenance (see the parable of the seed, Matthew 13:1-9; 18-23). Daily devotions are a vital part of the maintenance schedule.

A meeting in the throne room

P ROBABLY THE NUMBER ONE reason that most of us aren't enjoying a pattern of spending time with God is that we just don't know how to do it. We kind of sit there in front of our Bibles trying to find something we understand and we read a passage like ". . . and for the parbar on the west there were four at the road and two at the parbar" (1 Chronicles 26:18, *RSV*). It's kind of hard to pump yourself up about how helpful this is going to be!

If we actually thought that we were going to be ushered into the Oval Office to meet the president, most of us would find a way to crawl out of bed and get down there. The reason that we don't line up at the West Gate every morning is that we know it probably won't happen. The reason most of us don't get up a few minutes earlier to go into the throne room of almighty God is because we're just not all that confident we'll get to meet him.

Here are some practical tips that might help you turn good intentions into a consistent habit of spending time with God.

You need that special Quiet Time. If you're really serious about having daily devotions, probably the first step is to set up a time when you can do it. If you're going to spend some time with any other friend, that's usually the first detail to iron out: When will we get together?

Choosing a time to meet God is not some big, legalistic deal. It doesn't even have to be in the morning. It could be at night right before you go to sleep (just make sure that you don't do it *while* you're going to sleep), or in study hall at school, or during lunch, or even on the bus on the way to school (most people tend to pray a lot during that trip, anyway).

The length of your Quiet Time is completely flexible. We tend to think that God will like us better if we pray a long, long time and read all the chapters in the Bible. But that's not necessarily true. As a new Christian, I was always intimidated by those people who stood up in church and said with a superspiritual tone, "I rose this morning at 3:45 to meet God." I thought to myself, "Great . . . I rose this morning at 3:45, went to the bathroom, and went back to bed."

My suggestion is that you begin by allowing about ten minutes for your Quiet Time. That's not such a big bite that you'll choke on that kind of commitment. And that allows five minutes for reading the Bible and five minutes for prayer. As you desire more time, you can always increase it.

What usually happens, however, is that we get so fired up about the idea of having devotions that we start with this totally unrealistic commitment—"I'm going to get up tomorrow morning at 1:00 a.m. and memorize the entire Old Testament before school"—and we end up bailing out of the commitment by the second day. Like any smart runner, we need to pace ourselves realistically.

You need a place. One of the ways to build some consistency in your devotional life is to have a definite place to meet God each day. It can be in your room, at your desk, in front of a fireplace, or behind your house. The actual setting is no big deal. No one is suggesting that you build a little shrine in your bedroom with flowers, candles, this book, an Amy Grant album, and an issue of *Campus Life* magazine. It should be a place that is relatively private and it should be a quiet place. Having your Quiet Time while watching "The Lust Boat" on television and eating popcorn with your friends is not likely to be as effective.

You need a plan. When you first begin to have a Quiet Time, it's usually a good idea to have some set plan of what you are going to read and pray about. There are some great devotional guides for teenagers that can help you choose a passage to read and to think about what you've read. I recommend beginning with one of those. As you get more experienced, you may not need this kind of tool. Your youth worker or youth sponsor can help you with this, or you can probably just go to a Christian bookstore, tell them what you want to do, and they will help you find what you need.

For people who don't like to use written materials like this, it's probably a good idea to use a plan that includes reading about ten verses to a half chapter of the

Bible a day. The Gospel of Luke is a good place to start. The Book of Leviticus is a bad place to start. Don't worry too much about the passages you don't understand. Begin by concentrating on the ones you do.

What I do not recommend is the haphazard approach of letting your finger fall in the Bible and claiming this as your "Verse for the Day." This used to be my approach until one morning my "Verse for the Day" was 1 Samuel 24:3: "He came to the sheep pens along the way; a cave was there, and Saul went in to relieve himself." What a blessing!

You need a Bible. Surprise! Actually, not just a Bible; you need a Bible you can understand. Trying to understand a book that was written 2,000 years ago is hard enough. For most of us, ancient culture is quite different from what we're used to. The customs are strange. Most of the names are at least six syllables longer than the name of any kid we know at school. And the geography is totally foreign to us (no pun intended). If you tried right now, I'll bet you couldn't find Palestine on a map of South America. (That was a joke.)

Why complicate matters any further by reading a Bible that is written in a dialect that is awkward for you? Get a modern translation of the Bible you can understand. I don't speak in King James English and I seriously doubt if thou dost. Again, ask your pastor, or youth worker, for suggestions about which Bible to use.

Now that you have all the tools in place, it's time to start digging for treasure from the Word of God.

Reading the Bible for fun and prophets

S OME OF MY MOST awkward moments in junior high school came when we were all herded into the gym for dance lessons. You can imagine the passion in the air when the gym teachers volunteered about five of us seventh graders to each ask some poor girl to dance. Four out of the five of us were still convinced that girls basically had "cooties," so we weren't exactly romantic. We walked up and down in front of these girls looking for a partner with all of the tact of a sheik buying a camel.

Don't worry about the parts of the Bible you don't understand. Concentrate on the parts you do understand.

The worst part though, was learning the dance steps. One-two-three-slide, one-two-three-get off your partner's foot. You've been there. The gym teachers told us how wonderful it was that we could learn these necessary social graces, and how exotic it was to glide across the floor with our partners. Most of us, on the other hand, were so busy watching our feet that we hadn't even noticed we had a partner. To us, this ritual of romance and grace had been reduced to three steps and a slide. Shivers!

We can feel that same sense of awkwardness when we try to master the "mechanics" of a regular time with God. We hear the more mature Christians talk about their wonderful times of prayer and Bible study; meanwhile, we're floundering with "one-pray, two-read, three-be totally confused by what we just read, slide-fall asleep, back to one. . . ."

Obviously, there is a lot more to reading the Bible than just three easy steps, and no one is suggesting that just going through the motions of the following plan is going to necessarily usher you into the throne room of God. But, before you can run, you have to walk, and using the following simple plan might help you to read and better understand God's Word. It can really help if you build your regular Bible study around the three steps of **Observation**, **Interpretation**, and **Application**.

Observation. The first step in Bible study is simply reading and observing what the text says. For example, if you're reading one of the Gospel narratives (stories), you're going to ask: Who are the main characters? Where is the action taking place? What is the main thrust of the story?

On the other hand, if it's a passage from Paul's letter to the Romans, you're not really reading a story; it's more instruction. You're still going to begin with observation, but the questions will focus more on the main topic. What is being taught here? Is this an explanation or a promise or a warning or a specific set of instructions about how something is to be done? As you begin to desire more in-depth study of the Scripture, you may want to use a commentary to help you really dig into the cultural, geographical, and historical details that make the passage come to life. Again, your pastor or youth worker can be a good resource for this kind of supplementary material.

Take a minute now to read through Luke 19:1-10, and on a separate piece of paper, write down everything you can observe about this story. Read it through a couple of times. Read the story from the perspective of Luke, and then read it from the perspective of Zacchaeus. Then, read it from the perspective of the townspeople. Although we don't want to read something *into* the lines of Scripture, we shouldn't be afraid to read *between* them.

Remember that Luke is only giving us a sketch. You have to read carefully, and with imagination, to get the whole picture. Most of us read through the text so fast that we miss half of what God is trying to paint for us. "ForGodsolovedtheworldthathegavehis-onlysonsothatwhoeverbelievedinhimwouldnotperish-buthaveeverlastinglife." See what I mean?

Interpretation. Now that you've observed what the passage says, you're ready to think about what it means. That's the second step of interpretation. From your observation in Luke 19, you might ask, for example, what does Jesus mean ". . . the Son of Man came to seek and to save what was lost"? Who is the Son of Man? Was Zacchaeus lost? In what sense? Was he looking for hardwoods and ended up among sycamore trees? What does that mean, he was "lost"?

At this point, you may begin to ask questions about what this passage teaches. What is the lesson for today? If it's a promise, to whom is it being made? Are there any conditions? If it's a warning, who's being warned? Why? What would this truth look like in today's world? Sometimes, it's even good to rewrite the passage in your own words. That may help you to think through what the text is actually saying.

Application. The third step in Bible study is simply moving beyond the question of "What does it mean?" to "What does it mean for me?" How should I apply what God is teaching here? How would this truth look in my life if I put it into practice? This is where Bible study becomes a little less comfortable. We're actually expected to live this thing out. In the words of James, "Do not merely listen to the word, and so deceive yourselves. Do what it says" (James 1:22). If doing Bible study is a three-step dance, this is usually where our toes get stepped on . . . or where some of us sliiiiide.

Bible study is not just getting to know the Word of God; it's getting to know the God of the Word.

Going back to Luke 19, you might apply this passage by asking yourself, first of all, if you have been hiding from Jesus. How do I hide? Why? What keeps me up in the tree? Am I willing to "come down at once . . ." and welcome Jesus into my life? Into all parts of my life? Am I ever like those townspeople, judging and sneering from a distance because "there's no way God could love somebody as sinful as so-and-so"?

One final word of encouragement here: Remember that the bottom line in Bible study is not just getting to know the Word of God; it's getting to know the God of the Word. The method you use is not all that important. Worrying too much about the right method or the three steps is like staring at your feet so much that you forget to enjoy dancing with your partner. Don't be discouraged if your initial attempts at Bible study are stiff and awkward. Effective Bible study is a skill you will learn and develop over the long haul.

You've got a prayer

R EADING THE BIBLE is allowing God to talk to us. When we pray we talk to God. Just as with Bible study, there are some steps that will help us as we try to develop this relationship with God. And again, they may seem awkward at first, but in time they will help us to express and enjoy a real love for God.

Adoration. I remember one specific occasion when my wife-to-be wanted to express her love for me. Looking back, I think she meant to say that I was "priceless." But, what actually came out was, "Duffy, you're worthless." The important point was that I knew where her heart was.

Prayer begins with praise. We call it "adoration" because it comes from the root word *adore*. This simply means that we begin our prayers the way Jesus said to: "'Our Father in heaven, hallowed be your name . . .'" (Matthew 6:9). It is praising God for the fact that he is God, that he is loving, that he is eternal, that he never changes, and that he is gracious. God's not looking for flowery phrases here. We're not writing this in some heavenly yearbook: "Dear God, Stay just like ya are. You'll go far. Luv ya!" We're expressing to God our praise for who he is.

Confession. The next step in prayer is confession of sin. We confess our sins as a way of saying to God that we have disobeyed him and we recognize the offense of our disobedience. "Confession" comes from two words that mean, *to say the same thing as.* It's a way of saying,

"God, I know that what I did yesterday was wrong. You call it sin, and I call it the same thing. I'm sorry. Please forgive me. Erase the slate and let's start over."

When we pray a prayer of confession it should be specific, not some kind of industrial-strength umbrella prayer like, "Lord, if I've done anything wrong this year, I'm sorry." It is saying, "Lord, I know what I did. I know it was wrong, and I need your forgiveness."

Thanksgiving. Thanksgiving is when we put down our Bibles for a moment and eat some turkey. Okay, not exactly. Thanksgiving is when we give God thanks for what he has done in our lives. Adoration is praising God for who he is. Thanksgiving is praising God for what he does. Simple enough, huh?

Grace is when God gives us what we *don't* deserve. Mercy is when God doesn't give us what we *do* deserve. If you ever get in one of those slumps where you can't think of anything God has done to thank him for, take a moment to thank him for some of the things he *hasn't* done! I'm personally more thankful that God hasn't given me what I *do* deserve.

Supplication. When we first hear the word *supplication*, it sounds like it has something to do with food. "It's five o'clock, Mom. I'm hungry. Let's supplicate!" Actually, it comes from the word *supply*. It means asking God to supply our needs.

When we pray, Jesus said we should pray, "Give us today our daily bread" (Matthew 6:11). God is our heavenly Father, and he knows how to give good gifts. He loves us and wants to care for his children. What that means is that we can bring our needs to him, no matter how small or how big. He may not always answer the way we want him to, but what father does that?

In the words of Paul, "Do not be anxious about

anything, but in everything, by prayer and petition, with thanksgiving, present your requests to God" (Philippians 4:6).

Dance, children, dance

T HE WHOLE POINT of spending time with God is not to make sure that we've got all the steps down. Someday, we can hope, we will get to the point that we don't even have to watch our feet, that just as with any other relationship with a friend, our time with God will be spontaneous and natural. My prayer is that the instruction in this chapter can at least get us moving in the right direction.

Someday in eternity, we'll all enjoy a big party in the presence of God. We won't need Bibles and we won't need prayers, because we'll be with him. Won't that be something!? A party in the throne room of almighty God! I'll guarantee you that nobody is going to sleep through that one!

Chapter 5:
Keeping pace when
the going gets rough

WHILE STANDING THERE in the supermarket line, I was looking through one of those newspapers specializing in stories that reveal "shocking new reports" and "incredible new findings." There were the usual stories, "Bum's Smelly Feet Kill Wino in Homeless Shelter," "700-Pound Man Heaviest in World . . . and He's Looking for Love." But the headline that really got my attention was a classic: "Sunbathing Man Bursts Into Flames!" Wow!

Can you imagine? You're lying on the beach, minding your own business, when all of a sudden: *flame on.* When you come to, there are three little kids roasting marshmallows over your navel!

Most of us won't have to go through anything quite that bad, but there won't be any of us who go through life without occasionally getting burned. If it's not a problem at home, it's a problem at school, or a problem with friends, or a problem that is deep down inside that people don't even know about. Sometimes it has to do with relationships, and other times it's with money. Sometimes it's a physical problem, and other times it's some hassle with schoolwork.

The jungle that most teenagers run through on a daily basis has more than its share of wild animals, pests, and quicksand. Take, for example, a typical day in the life of a high school student.

You get up in the morning. For some of you, that's the first problem. Then, it's off to school. You're nailed in third period because you don't have your homework. That's another problem.

You say, "My dog ate it."

"You don't have a dog!"

"I know. My sister ate my dog." Another problem.

Then there's lunch, and, as everybody knows, there's no such thing as "school food" because *school* and *food* are two words that cancel each other out. So there's another problem!

Then, about sixth period, you have an argument with your boyfriend or your girlfriend. That's a problem.

Then, by seventh period, you begin to realize you don't *have* a boyfriend or a girlfriend to argue with. That's another problem!

Then, when you get home, there's more bad news. Your parents found out about the warning slip in English, and you're being grounded. They explain that you will be on restriction until you're married. Another problem.

How could any adult be so cruel as to promise you that "these are the best years of your life?"

Making the tough times tougher

SOMETIME BACK I READ A QUOTE that made a lot of sense to me. It sums up the way we all feel every now and then.

"Life is tough. It takes up a lot of your time. All your weekends. And what do you get at the end of it? I think that the life cycle is all backwards. You should die first. Get that out of the way. Then, you live twenty years in an old-age home. You get kicked out when you're too young. You work for forty years until you're young enough to enjoy your retirement. You go to college; you party until you're ready for high school. You become a little kid; you play. You have no responsibilities. You become a little baby. You go back into the womb; you spend your last nine months floating. And you finish up as a gleam in somebody's eye!" (James W. Cox, ed., *Best Sermons, Volume I* [New York: Harper & Row, 1988]).

Many of us have bought into the idea that people who really have it together don't have tough times.

One of the reasons that life sometimes seems so tough is that our culture has taught us some myths that make our everyday tough times seem even tougher.

"They lived happily ever after . . ."

F OR EXAMPLE, ONE OF THE MYTHS that many of us have bought into is the idea that people who really have it together don't have tough times. They just wake up each new day in one of those Disneyesque cartoon forests where all the animals and flowers are singing together, and the skunks are all cute.

The reason this myth is so convincing is that we live in a culture where no one wants to share their hurts and their problems. We don't like to be reminded of death and pain and hunger and loneliness. We want to hear about the *Lifestyles of the Rich and Famous*. We want to believe that these people never have any problems—that they jet from tropical island to tropical island living a carefree life where love is always good to them and their money can bribe away disease.

Unfortunately, it's not true. Although those of us living the "lifestyle of the poor and obscure" may find it hard to believe, no one escapes the pain of occasional tough times. Disney and Robin Leach can make it all seem so real, but it's just another fairy tale in Never Never Land.

Another common myth is that real Christians don't have problems. "If I were really the kind of person God wanted me to be, I wouldn't be going through this kind of mess. God must be punishing me. . . ." The tragedy of this myth is that it keeps us from going to the very God who can help us through the tough times. We feel like we can't run to God, because God is ticked off. He's the one who put us in this spot.

I recall leaving the breakfast table very quickly one morning as a little boy. I wanted to get out of the room and, if possible, out of the house before my brother began eating his breakfast. With uncharacteristic haste, I headed out to catch the bus and I slammed the door full force on my finger. I screamed. I cried. I held my hand and groaned.

Of course, moms are great under these kinds of conditions, so mine came over and started hugging me, kissing my finger, and telling me, "Bless your heart. You didn't deserve that, did you? You were just in a hurry to get to school. Poor thing, you didn't deserve that." And the more she talked, the louder I cried . . . because she didn't know what I knew.

What Mom didn't know was that before I left the breakfast table, I had put some pellets from the rabbit cage in my brother's Cocoa Puffs. I knew I *did* deserve it. I knew exactly what was going on here: God was nailing me for being a mean kid . . . and I deserved every single throb of pain I got!

It's not a myth that God gets angry. He does (Jeremiah 23:19, 20). Nor is it a lie that God sometimes punishes people. He does that too (Judges 6:1), although sometimes the worst punishment God could give us is simply to allow us to face the full consequences of our own bad decisions. The key is that when God does punish us, he does so as a loving, caring father who is trying to help his children, not hurt them (for more on this, see Hebrews 12:3-11).

The lie at the heart of this myth is that our tough times are *always* caused by our own sin and disobedience, and that's simply not true. Just because we're having tough times doesn't mean that God is angry with us or that we are not good Christians.

We might just be having tough times because life is tough. Good people get sick. Nice people face disappointments. The apostle Paul constantly faced some kind of hassle. Jesus was crucified. That doesn't mean they were being disobedient. In fact, sometimes the more we seek to obey God, the more we will face tough times. Jesus laid it right out: "In this world *you will have trouble*. But take heart! I have overcome the world" (John 16:33).

"It ain't over till it's over"

ANOTHER MYTH THAT HAUNTS US in our tough times is that life will never get better, that we could never *possibly* recover from the hurt and the pain we're feeling. If there is light at the end of the tunnel, it's probably a train!

> *God is bigger than our disasters. He really can make the crooked way straight.*

I remember feeling this way in eighth grade after my very first date. I was going to take Nancy Lipsy to an after-school basketball game. It was only a junior varsity game, but it was a big deal for me. It was my first real live date with a real live girl and I was petrified. That morning before school, I didn't just use Brut, I drank it! We're talking panic.

That afternoon by game time, I was beyond fear. I was virtually comatose with terror. What would I say? What should I do? What would she think? What about the guys? How come I'm not taller?

I met Nancy at her locker just after 3:00 and we made our way to the gym. I don't think I said anything until we got to the gym and all I said then was, "Would you like something to eat?" I think my strategy was that if we had food in our mouths, we wouldn't be able to talk and we wouldn't actually have to say anything. During

54

the entire first half, there was no time that I wasn't stuffing something in my mouth.

I still don't know exactly what happened. Whether it was just sheer nervousness, the hot lights and excitement in the gym, or all the junk I had eaten, I'm not sure. But one thing I am sure of is that with about three minutes and forty-five seconds left in the third quarter, the mounds of food I had wolfed down all afternoon decided that they had had enough of being crammed into a hot, dark chamber and took a quick and violent return voyage—all over Nancy. The bleachers emptied, people laughed and pointed, and Nancy decided not to ride home with me and my dad. It was a disaster that I figured would pretty much set me up for a lifetime of celibacy. I thought I would never recover.

But what I learned is that time is a great healer. We may be looking at a situation in our lives right now and view it with the conviction that nothing good can ever come from it. It's a disaster. "I will never recover. This is the beginning of the end." And yet, God is bigger than our disasters. He can make the crooked way straight. He can turn Good Friday into Easter Sunday!

Struggling with the big hurts

I WISH I COULD SAY THAT EVERY HURT and every trial was as simple as throwing up on my date, but we all know that's not true. Some of you reading these words even now are dealing with deep wounds—pains and problems that seem too deep and too severe for even time to heal. You're carrying the scars of sexual abuse that even years can't erase. You're feeling bad about your looks, or your weight—you've heard the cruel jokes and taunts from the other kids at school. You're suffering the ongoing pain of your parents' divorce that only seems to worsen as time goes by. You're held captive by an addiction to drugs or alcohol that, no matter how hard you try, you can't seem to break. A close friend of yours committed suicide last year . . . and maybe now you're struggling to find a reason to live.

I have a friend who never seems to hit her pace in her walk with Christ. It just seems that she cannot move forward for very long without be dragged down by some kind of struggle or depression. As we talked one day, we began to explore some of the issues she was struggling with, when all of a sudden she began to weep uncontrollably.

As we talked through her tears and her pain, she told me her story of being abused as a child, and how she had never, ever heard her father actually tell her that he loved her. As she spoke, I could hear rage and sadness and helplessness foaming out of this dark spot in her heart that she had corked up for almost ten years! No wonder she couldn't find the endurance for the race. She is still getting some help from a counselor, but, now, after almost a year, she is beginning to lighten some of the load that slowed her walk.

I wish I had a quick and easy answer to wipe away those tears, but I don't. No one does. What I do know is that each and every one of us is loved by God, and that this infinitely loving God is in control even when it seems he isn't.

God really loves you. He really does. Even when you can't believe it, he really does. And he will never give up on you. He will stay with you through your pain, grieve with you over your wounds . . . and he will be there, when you call for him and when you say, "Lord, I believe. Help my unbelief."

Someone has said that life is like a giant tapestry. From our perspective it looks like little more than a

jumble of threads, knots, and loose ends—and too often, those threads, knots, and loose ends have thorns
and barbs that cut and rip and wound. But God views
the tapestry from the other side. From God's perspective, and by his power, he is able to take all of those
loose ends and knots and threads—even the sharp,
jagged ones—and weave them into a masterpiece of
love. Sometimes, when all we can see is the tangle and
all we can feel are the barbs, we just have to trust God's
love for us, and let the Master weave his will.

The Olympic trials

E VEN THE BEST DISTANCE RUNNERS must first compete
in minor trial events before they are rewarded
with a chance to compete for the gold. Since people are
more interested in who is standing on the winners' plat-
form in the finals, these various trial events don't usually attract much media attention. What we tend to forget
is that every champion in the finals first began the race
in the trials.

Going the distance in the race with Christ is no different. Just because we are believers doesn't mean
we're granted a bye through the tough times. We all
have to run in the trials. In the New Testament, James
offers believers some instruction about how to press
on when we're feeling depressed.

> Consider it pure joy, my brothers, whenever you
> face trials of many kinds, because you know that the
> testing of your faith develops perseverance. Perse-
> verance must finish its work so that you may be ma-
> ture and complete, not lacking anything. If any of
> you lacks wisdom, he should ask God who gives
> generously to all without finding fault, and it will be
> given to him. But when he asks, he must believe and

not doubt, because he who doubts is like a wave of the sea, blown and tossed by the wind. That man should not think he will receive anything from the Lord; he is a double-minded man, unstable in all he does. . . .

Blessed is the man who perseveres under trial, because when he has stood the test, he will receive the crown of life that God has promised to those who love him. *James 1:2-8, 12*

This passage offers four key ideas for those of us running in the trials: **count**, **know**, **let**, and **ask**.

Count. James begins his instruction with the word *consider.* The word he actually uses is a mathematical term. Really what it means is *count.* "Count it all a joy . . . whenever you face trials of many kinds." Of course, our first instinct whenever we hear people say something like this is to punch them in the mouth. How can they be so ridiculous as to suggest such a thing? It's like the first time you watched Pollyanna. Here's this little girl going around to sick people and saying, "Let's play the Glad Game." It kind of made you want to play "The Vomit Game."

Actually what James is saying here goes much deeper than, "Don't worry, be happy. . . ." I never understood this verse until my little girl started playing violin. I think that experience gave me a new perspective on both joy and trials. Erin would stand in front of me performing her scales, hour after hour, playing her violin in a way that gave new emphasis to the name "vile-in."

What I began to notice was that during these little impromptu performances, she would get totally frustrated every time she made a mistake. Nine times out of ten, she would stop, sling her bow at the air, and then grumble, "That doesn't count." Every time she made a mistake it was the same thing: "Doggone it. That doesn't count."

Finally, one day we were in the middle of her practice and after about forty trips up and down the scale, she stopped to ask me a question: "Daddy, why are you drooling?" I hastily responded to her with an observation.

"You know, I've been listening to you play this violin now for over a year. And every time you've made a mistake, your response is basically the same. You get mad. You get frustrated and you yell out, 'That doesn't count.'

God can take all of our tough times and add them up into something that is an expression of his love.

"Well, I want to tell you something. I've been listening to you lately, and you know what? You're getting better. This is beginning to sound good.

"Do you realize what that means? That means that all those times you got mad and flustered, and said, 'That doesn't count'—you know what—it means they *did* count!"

That's what James is saying here to us in this passage. In the face of trials, we get mad; we get frustrated. We want to yell out, "That doesn't count." But what James is saying is precisely this: That all of these tough times do count, that an all-powerful God can take all of these tough times and add them up into something that is an expression of his love. James is saying that our trials might look like a loss for the moment, but that in the long run we should count it to the plus side of the ledger. "Count it all a joy. . . ."

Know. How can we do that though? What kind of heavenly calculation can make a negative situation into a positive one? Well, James gives us the reason for joy in the very next phrase: ". . . because you *know* that the testing of your faith develops perseverance."

Let's be honest, when we're going through hassles and bad times, there's much we don't know. We don't always know why. "Why did my boyfriend dump me?" "Why are my folks splitting up?" "Why can't I stop drinking?" "Why does God have to let my dad lose his job?" We don't know the answers to those questions.

We also don't know where and when we're going to come out of a bad situation. We don't know what God is doing behind the scenes on his side of the tapestry, or how he could possibly take this situation and use it for good. We don't know any of that stuff.

What we do know are these three facts. Number one: God is a loving God and he is in control. That doesn't mean that he's causing everything, but it does mean that none of it is taking him by surprise.

Number two: we know (James 1:3) that the "testing of [our] faith produces perseverance." What is perseverance? Basically, it's the ability to endure—the ability to go the distance. As any distance runner knows, there is no better way to build endurance than to get out there and run—to learn to overcome soreness and discomfort so that we can reach the finish line.

Anytime I take a group of students backpacking, I always face the toughest part of the trail in the first day, because that teaches them endurance. They begin to say to themselves, "Well, I made it through that day, I guess I can make it through this day." That way, by the third or fourth day, they can enjoy the adventure without having to wonder if they're really going to make it. By the fifth day, I might even offer to carry my own pack!

Number three, we know this: "Blessed is the man who perseveres under trial, because when he has stood the test, he will receive the crown of life that God has promised to those who love him" (James 1:12).

Obviously, the first question is, what is a "crown of life"? Any runner is curious about what kind of trophy will greet him at the end of the race. What is this "crown of life" business? Actually, it could be either of two prizes. The "crown of life" could be James's way of describing something that God gives us when we finally go to heaven, some sort of wonderful gift that we receive from the hands of God.

It could also be James's way of describing a mindset that is not intimidated by everyday life. It's a way of saying that by faith in God we can reign over the negative circumstances and situations we face in our everyday living.

I personally think that James means to say *both:* that there is a reward in heaven for those who hang tough through the race, but that we don't have to wait until the "sweet by and by" for our victory. As we endure trials, God gives us a special kind of victory even in the "nasty now and now."

There is a story told about a young boy playing a game of checkers with his grandfather. For the first few moves of the game, this little kid made several jumps and he was beginning to get a bit cocky. He started teasing granddad a bit, asking him if he was sure he could see the board okay. Finally, about ten moves and five smirks into the game, the grandfather reached over the board with this gnarled, bony hand that looked like an old tree limb. He picked up his checker and started moving across the board.

"Jump . . . jump . . . jump . . . jump . . . jump. . . . Crown him!"

With a big grin, he looked down into the face of his grandson and said, "Boy, don't ever forget this lesson. It's an important one. You don't mind getting jumped if you know you're headed for King Territory!"

We need to endure—not because we're so tough, but because we know who is in control.

That's what James is saying to us. There are going to be times in life when we get jumped. But we need to hang in there. We need to endure. Not just because we're macho tough guys, but because we know who is in control. We know we're headed for King Territory!

Let. One of my least favorite pastimes is going to the doctor for an annual physical. Maybe it's just me, but I find it a little awkward when I walk into an examination room and a perfect stranger says matter of factly, "Take off your clothes, please." I realize the nurse is trying to be businesslike, but the way she says it, I get the impression that she thinks I've been undressing in front of people all day. "No problem. I just finished undressing in front of everyone on the elevator. Just give me a minute."

And, then, while I sit in a room that has been chilled to a subzero level, I am told to make myself comfortable. You know the routine: first, the "Fill the Bottle" game; then, the "Bend Over and Cough" game. It's a barrel of laughs. That's why I occasionally get the sincere urge to grab the doctor's stethoscope and scream into it, "Hey! Hands off! You don't know me this well!"

There is, of course, a reason why I don't do that. There is a reason why I don't just push his hand away, grab my bottle and my clothes, and run for the door. The reason is simple: this doctor is doing what he is doing to maintain my health. If I do not let him do his work on me, I will risk some major problems down the road.

In a nutshell, that's exactly what James is saying about the way Jesus, the Great Physician, uses trials and tough times in our lives. "Perseverance must finish its work so that you may be mature and complete, not lacking anything" (James 1:4). When we're in the middle of trials, and the situation is uncomfortable, awkward, or even painful, we must fight the urge to squirm by reminding ourselves that God can use this situation to mold Christ-like character in our lives. But we must *let* him finish his work. God uses these trials not as daggers to stab and hurt us, but as scalpels, to operate in our lives and make us into the kinds of people he wants us to be, "mature and complete, not lacking anything."

Ask. Of course, the big question when we meet various trials is "Why?" "Why does a loving God have to use this particular trial to do his work in me? Why this? What is God trying to accomplish here?" Tough times always breed tough questions. It's no accident that James continues his instruction by reminding us that God is not offended by our questions.

> If any of you lacks wisdom, he should ask God, who gives generously to all without finding fault, and it will be given to him. But when he asks, he must believe and not doubt, because he who doubts is like a wave of the sea, blown and tossed by the wind. That man should not think he will receive anything from the Lord; he is a double-minded man, unstable in all he does. *James 1:5-8*

For most of us, the hardest part of going through hassles is dealing with all of the questions. Sometimes they gnaw at us gradually and sometimes they bite hard. James reminds us that the questioning is normal. There is nothing sinful or unfaithful about asking "Why?" In fact, we should ask questions in the midst of trials. That is often one of the few times when God has our attention long enough to actually teach us something. The only hitch is that we need to ask with the right attitude.

I remember asking my dad when I was a teenager if I could borrow the keys to the car. Inevitably, Dad would say something really funny like, "Yeah, you can have the keys, but we'd rather you not take the car." My dad was very funny.

When I finally realized he was serious and that I wasn't going to get the car, I wanted to know why. Now there were two possible ways to approach this investigative process. One was to say, "Okay, Dad, I know you're a loving father, that you care about my needs, and that you know it's not as romantic to walk my date to the movies. Why can't I borrow the car tonight? I'd really like to learn through this experience, 'cause, you know, I'm going to be a father some day, and I want to be responsible when I face this kind of situation. So, please, why can't I borrow the car tonight? Teach me, oh wise one."

That was not my usual approach. Unfortunately, my usual approach was a series of blurted, angry "Why's?" that neither sought nor expected any intelligent response. And, as you might expect, it made for a very short answer from my dad.

James tells us that when we go through trials there is nothing wrong with asking God, "Why." But we need to ask in faith, without doubting. One way of asking "why" is with an open hand that really desires information. The other way of asking "why" is with a clenched, bitter fist that just wants ammunition. That kind of questioning will poison us fast. We'll be like "a wave of the sea, blown and tossed by the wind." Your Father can't give you anything when you have that kind of attitude.

A gleam in your father's eye

L IFE IS TOUGH. It does take up all our weekends, and sometimes it seems to give us very little in return. There are days when it seems everything is backward. But what James shows us in this passage is that we don't need to be victimized by tough times. There is victory in a Jesus who has "overcome the world" (John 16:33).

> Who shall separate us from the love of Christ? Shall trouble or hardship or persecution or famine or nakedness or danger or sword? . . . No, in all these things we are more than conquerors through him who loved us. *Romans 8:35, 37*

On those days (or months!) when we're reminded of just how tough life can be, we can't afford to stop running. We need to **count, know, let,** and **ask**. No matter how bad it seems, you *are* a gleam in the eye of your heavenly Father, and together we really are heading for King Territory!

Chapter 6:
Watching your tongue:
Inviting Jesus into your mouth

W E'RE GOING TO START this chapter with a little "scratch and sniff" exercise. Here's what you do: Go into the bathroom, stand in front of the mirror, open up your mouth, and stick out your tongue. Take a look at it for a minute, and try not to let anyone see you. Then come back here to the book and we'll talk about it. Go ahead. I'll stay here.

Celebrating the tongue

M OST OF US DON'T THINK much about our tongues. No one feels a need to decorate a tongue or dress it. No one ever says, "Oh, I *can't* come over now. I just brushed my teeth. My tongue's all wet and I can't do a thing with it." We say stuff like, "Cross my heart and hope to die," but we never make a vow saying, "Cross my tongue and hope to choke." Mark Antony said, "Friends, Romans, countrymen, lend me your ears." Nobody ever opens a speech by saying, "Friends, Romans, countrymen, lend me your tongues!"

But, from God's perspective, your tongue may be one of the most important parts of your body. James describes it as being like the rudder of a ship. Boats are "so large and are driven by strong winds," but "they are steered by a very small rudder wherever the pilot wants to go."

> Likewise the tongue is a small part of the body, but it makes great boasts. Consider what a great forest is set on fire by a small spark. The tongue also is a fire, a world of evil among the parts of the body. It corrupts the whole person, sets the whole course of his life on fire, and is itself set on fire by hell. *James 3:4-6*

Ouch! I think what he means is that the tongue is pretty important. It has the potential for a lot of good, but it also has the potential for a lot of bad. Like a rudder, it sets the course for our lives. Most people don't even think about it, but essentially, it determines the direction we're going to take. If we intend to stay on course in our endurance race of faith, we'll need to better understand how what we say affects how well we run that race.

That's basically what Jesus was talking about when he said,

> Listen and understand. What goes into a man's mouth does not make him "unclean," but what comes out of his mouth, that is what makes him unclean. . . . the things that come out of the mouth come from the heart, and these make a man "unclean." *Matthew 15:11, 18*

In fact, when David wrote in Psalm 19 of God's handiwork in nature, and about the goodness of God's law, he finished out his prayer by talking about his mouth.

"May the words of my mouth and the meditation of my heart be pleasing in your sight, O Lord, my Rock and my Redeemer" (Psalm 19:14).

David sort of shucked it right down to two basic

areas of obedience, if we want to please God. One is the heart, and the other is the mouth. If we can bring these two areas under the lordship of Jesus, it will help us to go the distance with Christ.

Because this concept of taking our own speech seriously is so new to most of us, I have prepared the following poem to echo and affirm the gift of speech:

An Ode to Speech

Between your jaws and under your tooth
is an appendage appearing at first uncouth;
It's red and porous and mushy and wet,
but a tongue without a mouth is like a fisherman without a net.
Without a tongue, we wouldn't be able to eat,
all we would get is the taste of defeat.
You could buy your cereal and pay your money,
but all you would taste is "nuttin' honey."
Why even the tastiest morsel would be just a dud,
so open up your mouth and say, "Hey thanks, Bud."
(This line refers to taste buds.)
Your tongue has many uses, many of them whacko,
You can roll it, you can swallow, you can even chew tobacco.
The whole tongue is vital, it's crucial every inch,
some use it to Spanish, some use it to French.

The tongue is not for filth or profanity or worse;
we use it to bless, instead of to curse.
And to make that happen, there's only one hope,
and it isn't washing your mouth out with soap.
Your body's a ship, and the tongue is the rudder,
so make Jesus the captain, for there is no "udder"
("other"—poetic license)
As I complete this poem, this ode to speech,
I say to each his own, and to own his each (??).
I make this plea, and I make it not in haste:
If you're going to use your tongue, please do so with taste!

Speech in good taste

IN EPHESIANS 4, Paul gives us some pretty practical instructions about how we can make the best use of our tongues. It's a passage in which Paul explains what it means to "lead a life worthy of the calling" we've received as Christians.

> Therefore each of you must put off falsehood and speak truthfully to his neighbor, for we are all members of one body. 'In your anger do not sin': Do not let the sun go down while you are still angry, and do not give the devil a foothold. . . . Do not let any unwholesome talk come out of your mouths, but only what is helpful for building others up according to their needs, that it may benefit those who listen. . . . Get rid of all bitterness, rage and anger, brawling and slander, along with every form of malice. Be kind and compassionate to one another, forgiving each other, just as in Christ God forgave you.
> *Ephesians 4:25-27, 29, 31-32*

Paul gives us three specific guidelines for the ministry of the mouth in this passage. In each case, he tells us first what we should not do and then what we should do. He explains it as "putting off" the old, and "putting on" the new.

Part of what it means to lead a life worthy of our calling is that we go through both the "putting off" and the "putting on" process. If you're preparing for a date after a hard afternoon workout, it's a good idea to get cleaned up first. Put off the old sweaty stuff and take a shower. Very few people genuinely appreciate Eau de B.O.!

But, we can't stop there. Next, we have to put on some clean clothes. If you just step out of the shower and into the car without going through the "putting on" process, that could also cause some problems! That's what Paul is saying here. The Christian life is not just defined by what we "put off," but by what we "put on." The difference between legalism and the Christian faith is that genuine Christianity is never defined solely by what we don't do. We put off the old life of walking in darkness, and put on the new life of walking in the light.

Put away truthlessness

W E LIVE IN A CULTURE THAT HAS MANAGED to blur the line between falsehood and truth. Whether it's politicians or educators or ministers or bankers or athletes or the kid who sits next to you in English—it's hard to know whom you can trust anymore. If Pinocchio's curse was spread around, most of us would have enough nose to smell a *picture* of a rose. Paul cuts right across the grain of our modern culture when he begins this passage by saying, "put off falsehood and speak truthfully."

Our culture has managed to blur the line between truth and falsehood. It's hard to know whom you can trust.

What do we mean by falsehood? Does that include "white lies?" What about when we try to cover up for a friend in trouble? What about those "just-this-once" stories we tell to get out of a bad situation?

71

Well, it's really not that confusing. Essentially, we're talking about any kind of speech that might lead someone to a wrong conclusion. When we promise to do something and we don't do it, that's a lie. When we say that we did something we didn't do, that's a lie. When we say something that we know isn't true, that's a lie.

Of course, by the time we've reached high school, most of us have had a pretty thorough training in truthlessness. After about fifteen years, we've made lying into an art form. We get so very good at it that we're experts by the time we graduate from high school.

Check out the following conversation:

Liar #1: "You've finished that report that's due on Thursday, haven't you?" [TRANSLATION: "I haven't even started thinking about that report and I hope I'm not the only one."]

Liar #2: "Not quite." [TRANSLATION: "I think I may have picked a title for it, but I haven't done any of the research."] "How about you?"

Liar #1: "Well . . . not exactly." [TRANSLATION: "All I have to do is everything."]

Liar #2: "But Ted said you told him you were all finished."

Liar #1: "Well, just what do you mean by 'all finished?'" [TRANSLATION: "Okay, I lied to the guy."]

If we're not careful, we can get so good at this that we even learn how to lie by telling the truth. I remember one occasion during my junior year of high school. My parents had given me strict instructions one Friday night to be home by 1:00 a.m. That seemed fair enough until I met up with a bunch of friends at 12:45, and they said they were all going to Shoney's for something to eat. Suddenly, one o'clock seemed way too early and I decided to chuck my parents' game plan altogether.

Well, of course when I got home around two in the morning, my parents had long since gone to sleep. I sneaked up to my room confident that everything was cool. It wasn't till I came down to breakfast the next morning that I sensed all was not right. Both of my folks were sitting in the kitchen, and it was obvious they were not amused. Mom spoke first.

"Duffy, you know that we told you to be in by 1:00 last night, and you thought that was fair. Now, Dad and I were asleep by 12:30, but I just want to make sure that you were here in this house by the time you promised."

I knew that I had to think fast. I didn't want to just tell an out and out lie, but I didn't want to get in trouble either. I thought about using the old "Time Zone" strategy: "Oh yeah, Mom, when I came in last night it was well before 1:00 (in Hawaii)." Then I thought maybe I'd go for the "a.m./p.m." approach: "Now wait . . . did you guys mean I was supposed to be in by one in the morning? I thought you meant one o'clock Saturday afternoon."

Regardless of how we do it, lying is a sin. And the reason it's so serious is because of what it does to our relationships with each other. As Paul puts it, "Put away falsehood . . . for we are all members of one another." Have you ever thought about what would happen if one part of your body lied to another part of your body?

What if you reached out to touch a hot stove and your finger lied to you? "We're not getting burned. Don't worry." Then, all of a sudden, your nose tells you the truth: "Then why do we smell burning flesh?" What if your eyes lied to your legs about where you could walk? What if your ears lied to your brain about when it was safe to walk? It wouldn't be long before your body was either dead or severely paralyzed.

That's exactly what happens in our relationships when we don't put away truthlessness. People are afraid to reach out. They're afraid to move, because they don't know whom to trust. That is why Paul tells us to "speak truthfully to [our] neighbor" (Ephesians 4:25).

> *When we use foul speech, we're not just hurting ourselves — we're hurting everyone who hears us.*

Put away couthlessness

PAUL'S SECOND KEY IN THE MINISTRY of the mouth is, "Do not let any unwholesome talk come out of your mouths." What Paul is referring to is profanity, dirty jokes, racial slurs—basically anything that doesn't build other people up when they hear it. Here again, the Bible comes off sounding kind of prudish. Most of us today don't take that kind of standard seriously.

Fifty years ago, it may have been true that "Nice boys don't smoke, drink, cuss, chew, or go out with the girls that do." Nowadays, nobody thinks anything about launching a few four-letter words every now and then. It's just the way people talk. In the movie *The Breakfast Club*, I remember being disgusted by all the filthy language. When I realized that the film was just being realistic, I was even more disgusted. That's the way people talk.

But that doesn't mean that God doesn't take filthy language very seriously. He does. Because all of that verbal trash is just the tip of an iceberg of garbage down on the inside. Jesus put it this way:

> "For out of the overflow of the heart the mouth speaks. The good man brings good things out of the good stored up in him, and the evil man brings evil things out of the evil stored up in him. But I tell you that men will have to give account on the day of judgment for every careless word they have spoken. For by your words you will be acquitted [cleared], and by your words you will be condemned."
> *Matthew 12:34-37*

You see, when we use unwholesome speech, we're not just hurting ourselves, we're hurting all the people who hear us. The actual word that *unwholesome* comes from was the same word used in New Testament times to describe rotten fruit or foul fish that had been sitting out in the marketplace under the hot sun for several days. It stunk. It was spoiled. If you took it in, it could make you very sick.

That's the problem with foul language. We talk it. We listen to it. We take it in. We laugh at it. And before long, it becomes a standard part of our diet. We don't even realize it's causing problems, until slowly but surely it stunts our spiritual growth and makes us sick.

As wholesome as we wanna be

INSTEAD, CHRIST CALLS US TO SPEECH that builds us up. In other words, the standard for whether speech is unwholesome or not is whether or not it will build up the listeners. Does that mean we can never tell a joke unless it's spiritual?

"Knock, knock."

"Who's there?"

"Jesus. He said, 'Knock and the door shall be opened.'"

No, that's not what it means. Good, clean humor does build us up. It gives us a chance to laugh, and that's great. We just need to make sure that we aren't feeding each other some sweet, profanity-coated humor that tears down our spiritual health. That kind of blunder can very seriously slow us down as we run the race.

Put away ruthlessness

EVERY BIOLOGY CLASS IN THE WORLD has a chart somewhere on the wall that shows the growth and development of a frog. It always starts at one end and progresses through various stages, until at the far end of the poster there is a full-grown frog. Even as I explain it here, I think it's obvious why these posters get students so excited.

Paul uses this same kind of approach in Ephesians 4 as he explains why we need to put away ruthlessness.

> Get rid of all bitterness, rage and anger, brawling and slander, along with every form of malice. Be kind and compassionate to one another, forgiving each other, just as in Christ God forgave you.
> *Ephesians 4:31, 32*

What Paul shows us here is that sin starts small and grows big. No one starts out by just yelling insults at another person. That might be the way it looks, but that's not the way it happens. Ruthless language between two people doesn't just happen. It has a root. And that root is bitterness.

Bitterness grows down under the soil of the

heart. No one even knows it's there. We've all been told since we were little that "if we can't say something nice, we shouldn't say anything at all," so we try to deny that the bitterness is there. We try to cover it over with phony spirituality, but it just keeps on growing. Meanwhile, it progresses into rage . . . and then into anger . . . and then into *brawling* and *slander* and every form of malice! And by that time, we've used our tongues to say words that we will long regret, but cannot ever take back.

So what are we supposed to do?

We're supposed to deal with it when we feel bitterness towards another person. Talk it out. Talk to the Lord. Talk to the person. But, the worst thing we can do is go undercover, stew about it, and "let the sun go down while you are still angry." In the words of Paul, that gives "the devil a foothold" (Ephesians 4:26-27). In fact, Paul tells us that anger, by itself, is not necessarily a sin. It becomes a sin when we let it grow from bitterness into rage and slander.

The other important lesson from this passage is about that word *slander*. We need to understand that slander is serious business. When most of us think of slander, we think of sarcasm, sort of cutting someone down and then laughing it off. That's what we usually do, isn't it? "At least I'm not as _____ as so-and-so. . . . Just kidding."

What Paul shows us in this passage is that slander and sarcasm are not something we should kid about. We all know that deep down inside, anyway. We've all felt the pain of one of those "kidding" comments. It's no wonder that the word *sarcasm* comes from two words that literally mean *ripping the flesh*.

I guess we don't take sarcasm seriously because as children we were told that "sticks and stones could break our bones, but words would never hurt us." By the time we've lived a few years, we all know better. We've all felt the sting and the pain of a sarcastic barb that left everybody in the room but one person laughing. Sometimes, in reality, it's those kinds of memories that leave scars long after the stick wounds have healed.

We often refer to slander as a "cut down," or a "put-down," but God calls it worse. Actually the word Paul uses here for slander comes from the same word as *blasphemy*. Frankly, there was a time when that didn't make sense to me because I always thought of blasphemy as speech that was insulting to God. How could I be insulting God when I was just making fun of some geek at school?

It never made sense to me . . . until I got married. We were on our honeymoon, and my wife had made her first dish as a married woman. It appeared to be some kind of stew, but, honestly, it was anybody's guess without some sort of FDA report. With all the tact I could muster, I looked at it, and looked at her, and simply said, "Maggie, if this is a stew, it stinks." (I was good with words even then!)

Before I knew what had happened, she gasped, stood up, and ran from the room crying. Not having been married for more than a few hours, I couldn't understand the big deal. I hadn't said that she stunk. I just said the stew stunk. But that's when I learned my first lesson about marriage: When you insult the stew, you insult the person who made that stew. . . .

That's what Paul is saying here. When we slander another person, we insult the God who made that person, and loves that person, and sent his only Son to die for that person. And that is nothing less than blasphemy.

Forgiveness is the key

I T'S NO ACCIDENT THAT PAUL FINISHES OUT this passage by pointing us to forgiveness. The truth is that very few people can read through a passage like this without being reminded of words that have hurt them and words that they have hurled in return. More than likely, all of us have been on both ends of those bullets of blasphemy at one time or another. This is a passage that leaves none of us innocent. We've all felt the cuts and we've all fired the comments.

That means that forgiveness is the last order of business. We've got to end there and begin there because that's the only way to chop at that root of bitterness. Grudges always breed grudges. And we need to forgive others because we want them to forgive us.

We've all felt the pain of a sarcastic barb that left everybody in the room laughing but us.

The last words

I WONDER WHAT THIS MIGHT ALL MEAN for someone reading this book. Probably for more than a few of us, it means we have to undergo a major overhaul of the mouth. It's far too easy for some of us to slip in a word of deceit here or there and go right on running without realizing we've cut a corner from the course.

For others of us, a serious walk through this passage might mean we need to do some reevaluation of the kinds of things we consider funny.

For almost all of us, it will mean that we need to ask forgiveness—first from God, and then from a parent or a friend or a teacher.

When we read through a chapter like this, it's easy to feel the way Isaiah did that day when he caught a vision of the holy God in his temple. Isaiah just melted to his knees and said, "'Woe to me! . . . For I am a man of unclean lips, and I live among a people of unclean lips . . .'" (Isaiah 6:5).

If that's the way you're feeling at the end of this chapter, the great news for you is that God forgave Isaiah that day. He touched his mouth and said, "'See . . . your guilt is taken away . . .'" (Isaiah 6:7).

Why don't you take a minute to close this chapter by using Isaiah's prayer to talk to God about your own lips? He's ready and willing right now to touch our tongues, and to help us put away truthlessness, couthlessness, and ruthlessness.

Chapter 7:
Outrunning temptation:
Taking on the Devil's Triangle

I T WAS 2:10 IN THE AFTERNOON on December 5, 1945.
Five U.S. Navy planes took off in clear weather from
Fort Lauderdale, Florida, and flew east over the At-
lantic Ocean. Commanding Flight 19 was Lieutenant C.
C. Taylor, who was overseeing four student pilots and
their crews—fourteen men in all. By 3:40 that afternoon, Lieutenant Taylor reported that his gyroscope
and magnetic compass were not responding properly.

For the next several minutes, the four student pilots followed Flight 19 as their leader wandered aim-
lessly, first east, then west, then northeast over the
ocean as Taylor tried to get his bearings by radio. Then
suddenly, Flight Commander Taylor gave quick orders
to bail out, to ditch. It was only minutes later that all
contact was lost.

After the loss of contact, the Navy quickly dis-
patched two Martin Mariner giant seaplanes—aircraft
designed for long-range patrols—in the hope that they
might find the missing planes and their crews. After
several hours, the wind kicked up to thirty knots and
the visibility was so low that the seaplanes were or-
dered back to base. Only one of them made it back.

For days following, the Navy and the Coast Guard
combined to comb a 100,000 square-mile area with

more than 100 planes and surface craft. To this day, no one has ever found any traces of the planes in Flight 19 or the giant Mariner seaplane.

In the same mysterious way, two years later, on January 30, a British commercial airliner called the Star Tiger, with thirty-one people aboard, vanished after radioing Bermuda that all was well and that landing would be precisely on schedule.

More recently, on December 22, 1967, a twenty-three-foot cabin cruiser, the *Witchcraft*, disappeared off the coast of Miami after reporting propeller problems. The Coast Guard arrived on the scene within ten minutes of the first call, but no sign of the cruiser or its crew was ever found.

Similar episodes are found in government files regarding some forty ships and twenty planes that have disappeared over the last century within this area, described as the Devil's Triangle or the Bermuda Triangle, a geographical triangle that touches Bermuda, Puerto Rico, and a point in the Gulf of Mexico west of Florida. Many scientific and quasi-scientific explanations have been offered over the years to explain these incidents, but the best work on the subject is probably a 1975 book by Lawrence Kush, a librarian at Arizona State University. In *The Bermuda Triangle Mystery— Solved*, Kush logically explains each of the Triangle mysteries case by case. Basically, he exposes the "mystery" as a fascinating combination of hype, imagination, and folklore that really doesn't have much to do with Bermuda or the Devil.

The real Devil's Triangle

UNFORTUNATELY, WHAT LAWRENCE KUSH did not address is another devilish triangle that goes way beyond hype and imagination. It's a very real triangle that has caused more Christians to bail out and mysteriously disappear than any sector of world geography. And, most important of all, this triangle is no myth. All the librarians and books in Arizona couldn't explain this one away. It's a Devil's Triangle about which Scripture warns us with grave care and concern.

> *Nowhere in Scripture are we warned about the power of the Devil. Satan is real, but he is a defeated enemy.*

> Do not love the world or anything in the world. If anyone loves the world, the love of the Father is not in him. For everything in the world—the cravings of sinful man, the lust of his eyes and the boasting of what he has and does—comes not from the Father but from the world. The world and its desires pass away, but the man who does the will of God lives forever. *1 John 2:15-17*

Spooky stuff

J OHN DOESN'T WRITE ALL OF THIS STUFF to scare us. It's not as if some guy sat down 2,000 years ago and said, "Well, we have some pretty neat Bible stories for Christmas and Easter. Let's see what we can throw together for Halloween!" Nowhere in Scripture are we warned about the power of Satan or evil. It's true that Satan is real, and that he is our enemy. But Satan is a defeated enemy.

Jesus nailed him for good when he rose from the grave and conquered death. We're missing the point if we spend all of our time looking for Satan behind every rock and bush. His power can't defeat us. *But,* his strategies can. We've got to be aware of Satan's game plan if we're going to maintain our stride and outrun his tempting lures.

For that reason, John takes the time in this passage to introduce us to the Devil's Triangle of evil: the cravings of sinful man, the lust of the eyes, and the boasting of what we have and do. If you strip it down and call it for what it is, it boils down to passions, possessions, and pride.

Lust of the flesh

A H YES, THE "LUST OF THE FLESH." We've all heard of this. It's one of those subtitles that kind of makes you want to keep on reading. Essentially, it's what John is talking about when he writes about "the cravings of sinful man." Most of the time, when we think of the lust of the flesh, we think of sex and romance. (And most of the time, when we start thinking about sex, we stop thinking about anything else!) But, actually, the cravings of sinful man go way beyond sex. What this really refers to is the desire to do.

Yeah . . . that would probably include sex all right, but it's more than that. Actually, the word *lust* literally comes from two words that mean *over-desire*. Essentially, it's taking a God-given desire and overdoing it to the point that it begins to consume us. It's what we think about, joke about, talk about. It becomes our only focus. And that's not good.

For example, there is nothing abnormal or immoral about hunger. God gave us the desire to eat. We need to eat to stay alive. But, this same healthy desire for food can become an unhealthy desire that will kill us if we don't keep it under control. Just because we feel hunger doesn't mean we can go around scarfing every Twinkie, Dorito, and cheeseburger within 100 miles. That becomes gluttony, and God calls that sin because it destroys us.

In the same way, the drives for sex and romance are normal, God-given desires. They're God's gifts; not something dirty. I remember sitting in Sunday school in eighth grade and being told, "Sex is dirty . . . so save it for the one you love!" That never has been God's attitude about our sexuality.

However, Satan's strategy is to take this normal desire and con us to the point that we are consumed by it. It becomes the focus of all of our entertainment, all of our conversations, all of our thoughts, and all of our relationships. Guys become obsessed with steamy images of every imaginable sex act; girls spin romantic fantasies about the knight in shining armor who will swoop in and solve all of their problems with his strength, sensitivity, and sensuousness. Statistics say that the average teenager daydreams about sex once every fifteen minutes! (If that's true, then when I was a teenager, I think I spent the other fourteen minutes waiting for the next daydream.) It's almost impossible to do anything or go anywhere without being bombarded with distorted images of sex and romance.

Of course, some will say, "Well . . . what's so bad about that? It's better than being bombarded with geometry or participles or something." But, what's bad about the bombardment is that the lust of the flesh lures us to meet God-given desires in ways that God did not intend. And, even if you don't factor in all of the risk from sexually transmitted diseases, anyone can see from the rising divorce rate and from the increasing rate of premarital pregnancies and single mothers, that this kind of bombardment causes a lot of destruction and a lot of painful fallout.

> *Satan's strategy is to convince us that God is some kind of universal hall monitor.*

The weird part about all of this is that God comes off looking like the bad guy, like some kind of cosmic party pooper who is up in heaven taking names to make sure that nobody has any fun. In fact, God is the Creator of all pleasure. All Satan does is take God's good gifts and pervert them.

Just as an example, stop reading for a minute and write out the word *L-I-V-E* on a piece of paper.

Think of it as a word that represents God's plan that we might live with him, or, in the words of Jesus, "'. . . that [we] may have life, and have it to the full'" (John 10:10).

Now, take that same word and pervert it—write it backward. What does it spell?

Satan's great strategy is to convince us that God is some kind of universal hall monitor and that Christians are nothing but Victorian, overly moral prudes who just need to lighten up. But, don't believe the lie.

C. S. Lewis wrote a book in which he described various Satanic tactics by giving us a "behind the scenes" glimpse into the kind of training given rookie demons in hell. It's a great book, and one of my favorite sections is where this All-Star veteran demon named Screwtape gives instructions to his young demon trainee, Wormwood:

> "Never forget that when we are dealing with any pleasure in its healthy and normal and satisfying form, we are, in a sense, on the Enemy's ground. I know we have won many a soul through pleasure. All the same it is His invention, not ours. He made the pleasures: all our research so far has not enabled us to produce one. All we can do is to encourage the humans to take the pleasure which our Enemy has produced, at times, or in ways, or in degrees, which He has forbidden. Hence we always try to work away from the natural condition of any pleasure to that in which it is least natural . . . and least pleasurable. An ever increasing craving for an ever diminishing pleasure is the formula. . . . To get the man's soul and give him *nothing* in return—that is what really gladdens Our [leader's] heart" (C. S. Lewis, *The Screwtape Letters*, Revised Edition [New York: Macmillan, 1982], 41-42).

That's the way lust of the flesh works. When Satan confronted Jesus in the desert (Luke 4) he used the exact same strategy. Jesus hadn't eaten in forty days. He was hungry and he had a right to be hungry.

You can just imagine Satan's ploy: "C'mon Jesus, turn these stones into bread. Let's be reasonable . . . hunger is a very normal desire . . . God gave you these feelings. . . . Is it so sinful and bad to satisfy them? Does he really expect you to always go around hungry? What kind of God is that? That doesn't seem fair. What's so bad about a little bread?"

It's the same basic snare today that traps people just like us when we try to run the race. The more we get this time, the more we want next time—whether it's food or sex or any other desire. And the satisfaction that God originally intended for us always stays just one new relationship away, one more experience away. And God is the Scrooge who blocks our fulfillment.

The lust of the eyes

HAVE YOU EVER OPENED up a magazine or gone to a movie that had all of these beautiful bodies parading in front of your eyes and thought to yourself, "Boy, would I like to . . ."? No, of course you haven't. No way. Not at all. That's ridiculous! Although there may have been a couple of times. . . .

The lust of the eyes trips most of us at one time or another. If the "cravings of the flesh" are attacks from the inside, the "lust of the eyes" is an attack from the outside. It's not so much the desire to do, as it is the desire to have.

Again, when most of us think of the "lust of the eyes" we think of a bunch of seventh-grade guys hunkered down behind a library shelf thumbing through *National Geographic* and pointing to pictures of Samoan women, or watching Madonna strut around a stage with those weird cones on her chest. But again, lust of the eyes is more than just sex.

The story of Freddy Flounder

T O REALLY UNDERSTAND WHAT THE BIBLE means by "lust of the eyes," we need to step back and talk a little about temptation. What most people don't realize is that temptation itself is not the same as sin. It's no sin to be tempted. It's a sin to give in to temptation. Suppose you're watching TV, and all of a sudden, you see this hot little Italian number. The lines are in all the right places, the curves are pronounced, the look is sexy with a reputation for moving fast, and you decide right then and there: "I've got to have that car!" You watch the commercial several more times and each time you see it, you think, "Man, how can I get my hands on the steering wheel of that car?"

Then, what really makes it bad is when someone shows up at school with that very same car because "Popsy" gave it to him for his birthday. Now, it's the only thing you see when you drive into the parking lot. It's all you can think of when you see that person. That desire begins to hook you into feelings of resentment, jealousy, or envy. That car has become an object of lustful desire, and it's at that point that the temptation becomes sin. You start to think, "I've *got* to have a car like that!"

Or, maybe it's something completely different. You're sitting in your den doing your homework, talking on the phone, and watching soap operas. Beautiful people are walking around on the TV screen, people with names like Roman and Desiree. Suddenly, as the music begins to swell, the hunk and hunkette gaze deeply into one another's eyes, and the next thing you know, the hunk has the hunkette in his arms and is carrying her off into the sunset . . . no doubt to his palatial Hunkdome.

What happens? Your mind fades away to some knight in shining armor who is going to steal you away to some South Seas love nest where the bodies are always bronzed, the weather is always beautiful, and the guys are always sensitive. It's a wonderful daydream. In fact, it's so wonderful that some people visit that place every day, glued to that screen, lost in that soap opera, lured so completely by what they see that it begins to occupy their thoughts and their time. It's the "lust of the eyes"—the desire to have, and it can lure us slowly but surely into the Devil's Triangle.

Now, is it a sin to watch TV? No. Is it a sin to see something that appeals to us? No; we can't help how we feel. Is it a sin to find these things attractive? No; that's just the way we are. Well, when does temptation become sin? It becomes sin when we begin to see this car or that relationship as the object of our fulfillment, something we need to have to be content.

"But, I can't help it if these gorgeous cars/gorgeous guys (choose one, or both!) are cruising across the screen of my television set. . . ." No. You can't keep the birds from flying over your head, but you can keep them from making a nest in your hair. It is the "lust of the eyes" that draws us into longer looks, and then longing looks—and that's when we start to slide.

Now, the temptation to possess can reach into every area of our lives. We can lust after everything from clothes to jobs to grades to cars. Whether it's a car, a relationship, a blouse, or a pair of skis, if it begins to become the focus of our desire, it's still lust—not because God is some egocentric party pooper who has to get all the attention, but because he knows that that kind of desire might lure us into some bad decisions.

The eyes have it

THERE'S NO BIG SECRET for guarding against lust. The key is to watch your eyes. Eve fell in the Garden of Eden because she "saw that the fruit of the tree was good for food and pleasing to the eye . . ." (Genesis 3:6). David's tragic chapter of adultery and murder began when he was out on his roof one evening and he "saw a woman bathing" herself (2 Samuel 11). Satan tried to go for the eyes when he showed Jesus "all the kingdoms of the world" in the hopes of tempting Jesus to bow down before him.

There's no big secret for guarding against lust. The key is: Watch what you watch. Guard your eyes.

What it boils down to is simple: Watch what you watch. Guard your eyes. And, when you see something that starts to trigger normal, healthy desires, guard your mind. Remind yourself that God, and God alone, can meet your needs, and he will do it in a way that fits his will in his time.

For some of us, that may limit the kinds of magazines we read, or the movies and TV shows we watch. For others of us, that's going to mean we have to limit which places we go, or who we go with. It may mean we have to exercise some self-control in our thought life, or even in the way we spend our money.

Does that mean no more *National Geographic?* Not necessarily. But it probably does mean that we're only kidding ourselves when we buy the annual swimsuit issue of *Sports Illustrated* and expect it to inspire us to prayer—unless it's, "O Lord, how marvelous is your handiwork!"

The pride of life

RAISE YOUR HAND IF YOU'VE READ this far in the chapter and thought to yourself, "Man, I'm doing pretty good here. I'm not sitting around wishing I could do all kinds of sinful stuff, and I'm not drooling over all these things that I want to have. I guess I'm kind of like the Mother Teresa of my high school."

Unfortunately, if your hand is in the air right now, there's a good chance your nose is, too. That's why John finishes his description of the Devil's Triangle by talking about pride, about "boasting of what we have and do."

The only temptation more basic than the temptation to do and the temptation to have is the temptation to be. It's the pride of life, the temptation to think of ourselves as the center of our own little world. Really, it's the ground floor for all of the other stories of sin, because it makes correction and confession impossible. Even the Great Physician can't heal us if we're not willing to admit we have a need.

I remember one time in junior high school, I got some kind of allergy that made my face swell up like a big balloon. I couldn't speak at all, and I could just barely open my eyes, although I really didn't much want to, anyway. I wasn't really that psyched about hanging out with everybody when I looked like "Mr. Potato Head." And it wasn't very appealing to hear my friends come up and say, "Duffy, you're swell" and then start laughing.

That's essentially the effect of pride in our lives. In fact, the very word John uses to describe *boasting* is a word that means swollen or puffed up. Pride affects our ability to communicate with other people and it keeps us from seeing ourselves as we really are. And what's so scary about it, is that it's quite subtle. When we get a big head, we get mad at family members and friends who try to tell us we're running off course. Or, when we hear a Bible study, we think, "Well, I hope so-and-so is listening to this . . ." when, in fact, God might be trying to speak to us. It's really hard to keep running on course when we've been made deaf, dumb, and blind by pride.

Outrunning the Devil

L EARNING HOW TO DEAL WITH TEMPTATION before it deals with us can save a lot of pain. But, it's not easy. Scripture gives us some pretty good ideas about how we can outrun temptation before it outruns us. You might want to remember these tips the next time you feel the wind whip and start to blow you into the Devil's Triangle.

Don't set yourself up for an ambush. You know the areas that cause you the greatest temptation. A man going on a diet is a fool to take a shortcut through the bakery! If the best way to beat temptation is to avoid it, then the best way to avoid it is to know your areas of weakness and be careful not to set yourself up. Paul puts it this way: "Flee the evil desires of youth" (2 Timothy 2:22). Stay out of situations, conversations, and locations that might leave you vulnerable to ambush.

Remember, you're not the Lone Ranger. It must have been a good feeling for the Lone Ranger to know that he always had Tonto covering his flank. When the Lone Ranger was weak, Tonto was strong. When Tonto was weak, the Lone Ranger was strong. When the Lone Ranger was tempted to drop the mask idea, Tonto could be there to say, "Big mistake. You heap ugly, Kemo Sabe."

One of the most important steps in dealing with temptation is to think about the people you hang around with.

One of the best ways you can fight temptation in your own life is to commit yourself to a small group of friends who are willing to ask you the kind of hard questions that make you squirm sometimes. "Are you aware of how you come across to people when you talk like that?" "Isn't this the same kind of decision that got you into a bad situation before?"

Remember who your friends are. One of the most important steps in dealing with temptation is to think about the people you hang around with. There's an old saying: "If you sleep with dogs, you're going to get fleas!" If you start to feel yourself itch a lot, maybe it's time to start thinking about the kind of friends you have. Are they helping you in your walk with Christ? Or are they making it tougher? Paul warned in 1 Corinthians 15:33, "Do not be misled: 'Bad company corrupts good character.'"

Make up your mind before you're under pressure. Don't wait until you're in the backseat to start thinking about your sexual standards. When the heat's on and the hormones are screaming, that's not a very good time to start deciding how far to go on the first date! Those kinds of decisions are best worked out with the lights on . . . when you have time to think and time to pray.

Learn how to overcome without overkill. One of the reasons most of us walk so willingly into temptation and sin is that we just can't figure out a way of saying "No" to temptation without saying "No" to our friends. One of the best skills you can develop is the art of being honest and firm without sounding judgmental.

You may just have to level with a friend and say, "You know, I've got to be honest with you. I'm really trying to work on keeping my thoughts pure and my mind clear from always thinking about sex, and I'm just not strong enough to watch those kinds of flicks and still be the kind of person God wants me to be. Why don't we _____, instead? Okay?"

When all else fails . . . remember to read the Word and pray. That's the way Jesus overcame temptation (see Luke 4). If you keep in close touch with God through prayer and Bible study, it will be a lot tougher to wander too far without some bells going off. David wrote in Psalm 119:9 "How can a young man [or woman] keep his way pure? By living according to your word."

Basically, what that means is that the best defense is a good offense. Don't spend your time running away from Satan and temptation. Think in terms of running toward Jesus and his righteousness (2 Timothy 2:22).

Remember that God is on your side. He's the Rock on which we stand, and he's the God who forgives us when we fall. That's good news!

No temptation has seized you except what is common to man. And God is faithful; he will not let you be tempted beyond what you can bear. But when you are tempted, he will also provide a way out so that you can stand up under it. *1 Corinthians 10:13*

Chapter 8:
The home stretch:
Relating to your parents

GOING THE DISTANCE with Jesus seems like a good idea to most Christian students until we start talking about living out the Christian life in our own homes. All of a sudden, "going the distance" seems like an attractive option, but now we're sort of thinking in terms of running away!

The hardest place for most of us to live out our Christian witness is in our own homes, among those people who know us as no one else does. Our families see us when we're tired or depressed—when we're not as careful to be on our best behavior.

Our families watch us go away on a work project to clean up an inner-city playground, and leave behind a bedroom that has fungus growing on the walls. They hear us sharing our faith with a friend on the telephone and then yelling, "Hang up, brat!" to the little brother who picks up the other phone without knowing it's being used. It's hard to convince our parents that we're serious about running the race for Jesus when they can't get us to run a twenty-minute errand. It's been observed that we really don't know someone unless we've seen what's on the walls of his or her bedroom and had to share a bathroom for at least three days! There's some truth to that. It's at home that we show our true colors, and frankly, sometimes they're a bit faded.

Maybe that's why so much of the Scripture is devoted to families: family stories, family illustrations, family breakdowns, and family instructions. Over and over again, God makes it clear that the real test of faith is not whether we're willing to die for Jesus, but whether we're willing to live for Jesus. And the toughest place to live for Jesus consistently is in our own homes. Going the distance with Jesus is wonderful, but how can we successfully navigate the home stretch?

PRACTICAL IDEA NUMBER ONE

Sit down some evening and write a letter as if it were from your parents. Pretend they are writing a letter to their children about why they are running away from home. It might help you to look at life a bit more clearly from their perspective and begin to see them as real people.

Somewhere between *Cosby* and *The Simpsons*

NONE OF US LIVES IN THE PERFECT FAMILY. It would be great if we could come home from school and walk into the Cosby household every afternoon, but that only happens in televisionland. This chapter is not about how we can make our families into a *Leave It To Beaver* household or an *Ozzie and Harriet* home. It's about some personal steps we can take to make our less-than-perfect families better. It boils down to three main ideas: treat your family members like real people, take the initiative, and communicate.

Treat your family members like real people

"BUT, THEY'RE NOT REAL PEOPLE . . . they're my parents!" We tend to think of our family members in terms of what they do, as opposed to who they are. Mom is a cook and a chauffeur. She keeps everybody on schedule and worries about us eating junk food. Dad is a drill sergeant. He sort of barks out the orders to make sure chores get done: "Mow the lawn and cut the grass; Wash the car and do it fast. . . ." Little brother is a pest. That's sort of his spiritual gift. He doesn't do anything special.

It's important to realize that behind each of these stereotypes is a real person just like us. And, these real people have real needs, real hopes, real concerns, real plans, and real feelings just like us. We all want to be treated with this kind of thoughtfulness, but we're not as eager to grant others this gift of openness. Our normal response to family turmoil is, "You guys don't ever try to see things from my perspective. You don't ever try to understand what I'm going through!"

But what about Dad? Maybe the reason he seems tense and uptight so much of the time is because he's worried about money. He wants to make sure there is money for luxuries like a college edu-

It would be great if we all lived in the Cosby *household, but that only happens in televisionland.*

cation, and essentials like $50 tennis shoes and $60 jeans.

One recent survey estimated that raising a child through the first eighteen years of life costs about $150,000. Of course, most of you are thinking, "Ah yes, but at that price, I am a bargain!" And that's true, no doubt. But it's still a lot of money and a lot of pressure. We get angry because Dad is working when we want him to be around for something; but then we get mad when Dad says we don't have enough money for a new car. C'mon, Dad, get your act together!

PRACTICAL IDEA NUMBER TWO

Ask your mom or dad out for a "date," or maybe just a once-a-week breakfast. Don't ask for money. Just tell them two or three things that are important in your life right now. Then, ask them to do the same.

How about Mom? Sometimes she seems kind of quiet, sort of sad. How come she can't snap out of this mid-life funk? Maybe it's because Mom is beginning to realize that she is growing older, that her children are growing up and away from her. Maybe she's beginning to realize that now there are wrinkles and stretch marks where there used to be beauty marks. Maybe it's a little discouraging when she puts the Jane Fonda workout video in the VCR, and the screen just says, "Get Real!"

Maybe your little brothers or sisters act like they do because they just want some attention from an older brother or sister they look up to and admire. Maybe that sister in the next bedroom wants to be asked about deeper issues of life instead of, "Can I borrow your green sweater and your purple jeans?"

When we're going through our own moods, we expect other family members to be understanding. But when those same family members go through their moods, they are "moody" or "having a pity party." When we need to be forgiven for coming in late, we expect to be greeted with understanding and grace. But when we've been waiting in front of the school or the church for twenty minutes because a parent got caught in traffic, we expect them to "plan ahead next time." When we need to borrow some clothing or money from a brother or sister, sharing just seems "like the family thing to do." But when that brother or sister wants to borrow something from us, it's, "What do I look like? The Salvation Army?"

PRACTICAL IDEA NUMBER THREE

Host an open house in your bedroom one night and invite all your family members. Serve some punch and snacks. Just tell everyone to make themselves at home.

Take the initiative

IN A RECENT STUDENT SEMINAR we did an experiment. Two girls and one boy were invited to the front of the room where they were given instructions. The girls were each told to grab one of the boy's arms and start pulling in opposite directions. It was kind of funny at first, because when these two good-looking girls grabbed the boy's arms, you could more or less read his mind: "You know, church isn't so bad after all!"

As the girls started to pull, though, the situation

became a bit more interesting. Kids in the group started cheering for the girls. "Rip him up, tear him up. . . ." It was good, clean, youth group fun.

The amazing part of the episode was what happened. When the girls started to pull this boy's arms in opposite directions, he seemed instinctively to realize, "Wait a minute: They're going to pull my arms out of my body. That will be painful. I don't want them to do that!" and he began his own countermaneuver. He started pulling in his arms so that the girls were drawn closer together. In short, rather than face the pain of a split, he took the initiative.

> *You can take the initiative in many ways; it just takes a little muscle, determination, and imagination.*

That's really what I'm suggesting here with regard to family relationships. There is no question that there are forces in today's culture that threaten to pull our families apart. Whether it's the pressure of finances, jobs, schoolwork, stress, busyness, or any of a hundred other forces, most families are beginning to feel stretched. In most cases, there is little we can do about these situations. They are out of our control.

But there is something we can do to fight the pain of the split—and that is to take the initiative. We can begin to pull the family together. We cannot change the ripping force of an alcoholic parent, or

The People Who Brought You This Book...

Invite you to discover MORE valuable youth ministry resources.

Youth Specialties offers an assortment of books, publications, tapes and events, all designed to encourage and train youth workers and their kids. Just check what you're interested in below and return this card, and we'll send you FREE information on our products and services.

Please send me FREE information I've checked below:

☐ The Complete Youth Specialties Catalog and information on upcoming Youth Specialties events.

Name _____

Address _____

City _____ State _____ Zip _____

Phone Number ( ) _____

The People Who Brought You This Book...

Invite you to discover MORE valuable youth ministry resources.

Youth Specialties offers an assortment of books, publications, tapes and events, all designed to encourage and train youth workers and their kids. Just check what you're interested in below and return this card, and we'll send you FREE information on our products and services.

Please send me FREE information I've checked below:

☐ The Complete Youth Specialties Catalog and information on upcoming Youth Specialties events.

Name _____

Address _____

City _____ State _____ Zip _____

Phone Number ( ) _____

Call for fast service:
(619) 440-2333

BUSINESS REPLY MAIL
FIRST CLASS   PERMIT NO. 16   EL CAJON, CA

POSTAGE WILL BE PAID BY ADDRESSEE

YOUTH SPECIALTIES
1224 Greenfield Dr.
El Cajon, CA 92021-9989

Call for fast service:
(619) 440-2333

BUSINESS REPLY MAIL
FIRST CLASS   PERMIT NO. 16   EL CAJON, CA

POSTAGE WILL BE PAID BY ADDRESSEE

YOUTH SPECIALTIES
1224 Greenfield Dr.
El Cajon, CA 92021-9989

a brother who is doing drugs. We cannot change their behavior. What we can do is change our response to their behavior—not just react, but proact. That's taking the initiative.

PRACTICAL IDEA NUMBER FOUR

Plan a special evening for your parents. Prepare a nice candlelight dinner for them. As they get home from work, meet them at the door wearing a coat and tie and usher them in for hors d'oeuvres. Have your parents' favorite elevator music playing in the background. If you play a musical instrument, stroll through the dining room periodically serenading them. By the time the evening is over, your parents will be thoroughly convinced you are not their child.

Dinner Drill. I don't know about your family, but when I was growing up, there were a few unwritten rules at the dinner table. They weren't the kind we ever discussed as a family. They were the kind you more or less learned by trial and error. One unwritten rule was that certain kinds of jokes were not appreciated. "Hey, Mom, this doesn't look like pot roast. It looks like roast pot! Yuk, yuk, yuk. . . ." This kind of humor was not embraced at our table.

PRACTICAL IDEA NUMBER FIVE

Set aside a Saturday and offer to be your dad's "Slave for a Day." The only condition for your free labor is that he work with you on any project he assigns you to do.

Another rule was that no rude body noises were tolerated at the table. "Who thinks I can play 'Jingle Bells' without using my mouth?" Again, there was no audience for this kind of talent around our table.

PRACTICAL IDEA NUMBER SIX

Instead of driving the car down to the fumes and returning it to your parents without enough gas to pull out of the driveway, put gas in the car and pay for it yourself. (Maybe you can get your folks to show you where to put in the gas.)

One of the most important unwritten rules at our dinner table was: Never get up in the middle of a meal. It wasn't so much because of my parents' disapproval, as much as it was the fact that you might never make it back to your chair. As soon as anyone so much as nodded in the direction of the kitchen, people would start yelling, "Oh yeah, while you're up. . . ." It was dangerous. "While you're up, would you mind bringing the butter, pouring some more tea, and washing the car?" Even if we had to go to the bathroom, we just sat tight until the end of the meal.

PRACTICAL IDEA NUMBER SEVEN

Write your parents a letter telling them how much you love them. Sometimes it's easier to put your thoughts on paper than it is to actually speak them. If you can't find a paper and pen, just paint your message on the wall of their bedroom.

I can just imagine what might have happened if I had simply decided to take some initiative and show some kindness around my house.

Me: "I'm going to the kitchen. May I get anybody anything?"

Dad: "Yes, Son, would you bring your mother some smelling salts? She just passed out here at the table."

PRACTICAL IDEA NUMBER EIGHT

Get a cassette player and a blank cassette. Record a message to your dad about how much you love him and appreciate him. Put it in his car cassette player with the tape turned on and cued to the right spot. The next morning, when he gets in the car and starts up the ignition, he will hear this voice saying, "Good morning, Dad. Can we talk?" Extra Credit: Time your tape so that it is actually synchronized with your dad's drive to work. "Right about now, Dad, you're passing that old park where you taught me how to throw a Frisbee. . . ."

Making the First Move. You can take initiative in many ways; it just takes a little muscle, determination, and imagination. For example, you can take the initiative in relationships. If your family isn't spending enough time together, plan to have at least one meal a day together by coordinating schedules, by helping with preparation, and by making sure that everyone slows down long enough to gather around the table.

Another way of taking initiative around the house is by serving other people. Instead of waiting for someone else to get up and adjust the volume, answer the phone, bring some more gravy, stoke the fire, and bring Kleenex, we can make the first move. Sure, at first it seems like you're breaking a law of nature or something, but this kind of servanthood is contagious.

Communicate

I NEVER CEASE TO BE AMAZED by students in the youth group who go away on a retreat, have an incredible encounter with God, stand up on the last night of the camp, and just literally spill their guts to all of us around the camp fire.

PRACTICAL IDEA NUMBER NINE

Get seven small pieces of paper and write on each of them a brief message of thanks and appreciation to your mom for all the work she does around the house like cooking and washing clothes. Then, for seven days straight, stick one of these little notes in a pocket of your dirty clothes.

Imagine your mom going through the pockets of your dirty clothes and finding a note that reads: "Dear Mom, Thanks for washing this grubby pair of jeans again." For weeks she will be going through all your grungy clothes!

"I just . . . want . . . to thank you guys . . . for making this the best week of my life. The Lord has shown me . . . how really fortunate I am . . . to have such great parents who . . . love me . . . even when I act like a . . . jerk . . . sometimes. I don't know . . . I guess . . . like . . . I don't . . . talk to them enough. . . ."

Then, the next day, when we get back home and their parents meet them in the church driveway, they have all the eloquence of Neanderthal Man.

Dad: "Well, son, welcome back. How was the retreat?"

Son: "Uhgm."

Mom: "Was the food okay, honey?"

Son: "Uuuugh."

Dad: "Well, was it a neat camp—a good facility?"
Son: "Hmm."
Mom: "Did you meet any cute girls?"
Son: "Hmmmmmmmmmmmmmmmmmmm."

What's really incredible is that this same kid will come to my office in three weeks complaining that his parents don't understand him! I'm tempted to say, "Of course they don't. They're not pigs. Get a mouth, buddy."

It happens a lot in families, doesn't it? Everybody talks and nobody communicates. There are at least two areas in which most families can improve their communications. One is in the area of expression of love and appreciation. The other is in the area of their expression of confession and forgiveness.

PRACTICAL IDEA NUMBER TEN

Try saying, "I'm sorry." If we could allow this simple truth to invade our family relationships, it would make an incredible difference!

It's appalling how many family members never actually hear another family member say, "I love you." What a shame! Some of us are like the old man who had been married to his wife for forty-eight years and for forty-seven of those years had never told her that he loved her. When his best friend finally asked him one day, "How come you never tell Myrtle that you love her?" the old guy just answered, "Look, I told her forty-eight years ago that I loved her. Now, if I change my mind, I'll let her know."

One of the first and most basic ways that we can strengthen our families is by taking the time and making the effort to express affection to other family members. It doesn't always have to be verbal, or mushy, but we need to get in the habit of communicating our love.

Gettin' better all the time

N ONE OF US IS ALWAYS LOVABLE. And no one knows that better than the people who live with us day in and day out. They see us at our best and they see us at our worst. A family is a group of people who love each other more than they deserve. Yours may not be a perfect family, but you can make it a great deal better.

> Therefore, as God's chosen people, holy and dearly loved, clothe yourselves with compassion, kindness, humility, gentleness and patience. Bear with each other and forgive whatever grievances you may have against one another. Forgive as the Lord forgave you. And over all these virtues put on love, which binds them all together in perfect unity. *Colossians 3:12-14*

Chapter 9:
Mapping the course:
Making wise decisions

I LIKE THESE NEW BOOKS that are on the market that allow the reader to make choices as he or she reads through the book. One of the popular versions of this genre of books is the *Choose Your Own Adventure* series (New York: Bantam Books, 1984). The front cover promises, "You are the star of the story! Choose from twenty-two possible endings!"

For example, if you turn to page ninety, you have two options: If you want to charge into the dragon's den and face a fire-breathing dragon you turn to page ninety-seven; or, if you want to stay at the mouth of the cave and challenge a hundred screaming dwarfs carrying poisonous arrows, you turn to page 103; or, if you just don't want to hassle with it, you can rip up the book. It's great!

I am from the generation that learned to read using the Dick and Jane books. It was a whole different ball game back then: "See Dick run. See Jane run. See Spot run. See Dick and Jane clean up a spot where Spot ran. . . ." It's not hard to see why this stuff kept everyone on the edge of their chairs!

I think what makes this *Choose Your Own Adventure* series so fascinating is that it takes our decisions seriously. Our choices actually count. And, of course, what's fun about the dragon's den is that if you happen

to make the wrong choice, it's just a children's story—
you can start all over again. Or, you can close the book
and turn on the TV.

What most of us want more than anything else in
life is the chance to make our own choices, to shape
our own decisions. It's one of the great parts about
growing up. People start to take our decisions seriously. But, it can also get kind of scary sometimes, can't it?

Real life is no fairy tale. Every decision really does
count. We face real choices and real consequences.
And unlike the dragon's den, life doesn't always offer
us a second chance. Each decision we make today affects the chapters in tomorrow's story. We don't have
the option of coming back in nine months or ten years
and saying, "Let's do that one again." That is the sober-
ing part of making our own decisions. We actually have
to live with these choices. Take, for example, this real-
life African adventure.

> "It's a rainy morning in the Veronga Volcanoes
> of central equatorial Africa, and I'm crawling along
> on my hands and knees, nearly certain that some-
> where up ahead I'll intercept a family of twelve
> mountain gorillas. I'll want to move slowly now, care-
> fully. Blundering into the midst of them is so aggres-
> sively impolite that the dominant male might feel
> obliged to charge. I don't want to provoke a charge
> because I'd be disrupting the animals' lives. . . . In
> the event of a charge, I would have to do something
> very difficult, indeed. I would have to stand rock
> steady in the face of 500 pounds of rampaging, im-
> placable rage. I would have to stand there stupidly
> staring down a silverback gorilla because twenty
> years of research indicates that a gorilla almost nev-
> er makes contact with a human that holds his
> ground.

"On the other hand, if there's a forest elephant at the end of the trail, I should be prepared to run. I've been informed that elephants, unlike gorillas, seldom come pounding after a running man.

"Mostly, I don't want to encounter a forest buffalo. It's early for these guys. They don't usually get too rambunctious until about two hours before sundown. But you never know. The scientists and game wardens have told me that it does no good to hold your ground before forest buffalo because they will gore and stomp and kill you. Unfortunately, they also have a tendency to run down retreating humans, whom they gore and stomp and kill. Climb a tree and they will knock it down so they can gore and stomp and kill you. Some few humans have survived a buffalo attack by playing dead. They were merely gored and stomped in a playful, nonlethal level" (Tim Cahill, "The Jaguar Chronicles," *Outside* [October 1987], 13).

> *What most of us want more than anything else in life is to make our own choices, to shape our own decisions.*

It's not always easy to know which way to go in life. Even people who are committed to going the distance with Jesus can find themselves lost and off course. "Should I or shouldn't I?" "What are my options?" "How do I figure out what God wants me to do?" Sometimes we feel as if we're standing in the midst of an African jungle and none of our options looks very appealing. No matter what we do, we feel as if we're destined to be gored and stomped and killed.

Making wise decisions

> Trust in the Lord with all your heart and lean not on your own understanding; in all your ways acknowledge him, and he will make your paths straight.
> *Proverbs 3:5, 6*

T HE WRITER OF PROVERBS reminds us that making wise decisions basically comes down to our willingness to trust an all-powerful, all-knowing Lord, to place our future (and our present) decisions into his hands. That does not mean we'll always make smart choices. What it does mean is that a sovereign, loving God can somehow redeem even our occasional stupid choices and make our crooked paths straight.

There are some steps we can take as we walk through this maze that will help us guard our way and stay on track. Let's take a look.

Know Where the Light Is Coming From. It's impossible to make wise decisions if we don't have some kind of standard for judging right and wrong. In our culture today, we've been told that there is no such thing, that all of that morality stuff is as old-fashioned as bobby socks and penny loafers. It just doesn't work any more to talk about ideas like right and wrong, sin and righteousness, light and darkness, truth and falsehood. Today's morality is not "true-false," it's "multiple choice."

I saw a woman not long ago on a quiz show. She

was asked, "Which do we need the most, the sun or the moon?" She thought about it for a moment, and then, with a sparkle of enlightenment, she answered, "We need the moon the most! It shines at night when it's dark. And during the day when the sun is shining, it's light, anyway." (Could you try to remember to pray for this woman?) What is scary is that, at first, it made sense to me.

We cannot make smart choices if we don't know where the light is coming from, or if we lack convictions of right and wrong. We can't stay inbounds if no one has marked the boundaries. We don't know which side to drive on unless someone sets some guidelines. And when we start to lose these boundaries and guidelines and standards, it's like trying to nail whipped cream to a barn door. There's just nothing solid to work with!

When we don't have any set standard, we tend to get squeezed into the world's mold—we start to conform to whatever people around us say is right. We begin to have our path directed by whoever is the most persuasive at any given time. So, when we're around our friends at school, they shape our standards. When we're around our parents, they shape our standards. When we're around the youth group at church, it shapes our standards. We become chameleons who change "convictions" depending on our surroundings.

That's why we have to start with standards. This is a crucial first step. We have to begin with some basic convictions about where the light is coming from and set our path accordingly. David wrote, "Your word is a lamp to my feet and a light for my path" (Psalm 119: 105). We can follow the Word of God or we can follow the words of men, but we can't do both. The Bible puts it this way, "Do not conform any longer to the pattern of this world, but be transformed by the renewing of your mind. Then you will be able to test and approve what God's will is—his good, pleasing and perfect will" (Romans 12:2).

Don't Be Fooled by Appearances. It all looked innocent enough. The party was sponsored by a national charity, so it seemed like a good cause. The guys who were lined up at the kissing booth were psyched. The sign over the booth read, "Kisses—One Dollar." What a deal! A great-looking woman stood behind the booth, donating her lips for charity. Who could resist "A bucker for a pucker?!"

A temptation that seems harmless can turn out costing you a lot more than you bargained for.

It all seemed like a bad dream, however, the next morning when the local newspaper ran the headline, "Kissing Booth Volunteer Found To Have Hepatitis." But it was real enough. The county health commissioner advised all those who had stopped by the booth to go immediately to a community health clinic for a $5 injection that would lessen the threat of the dangerous disease.

Life plays those

kinds of games with us sometimes, doesn't it? You see a situation that looks great—so tempting—very attractive, incredibly appealing, and harmless. And then you end up making a decision that you regret later on—a decision that turns out costing you a lot more than was advertised.

The second step in making wise choices is not to be fooled by appearances. That's not easy in a culture where we've learned to make choices on the basis of goosebumps, rather than on the basis of good sense. The media, Madison Avenue, and big business conspire to paint pictures for us that are just too good to resist. In a world where we have a floor cleaner called "Glory" and a dishwashing liquid called "Joy," you know it's going to be hard to get a straight answer.

Sometimes the pretty lies come wrapped in music. Sometimes they just come "rapped." Sometimes the deceitful images come to us in the the movies we watch, or in the books we read. Sometimes the enticement just comes to us through the words of a friend.

It often seems very innocent. "These messages don't affect us." "I listen to the music, but I'm never affected by the words. . . ." "These kinds of movies don't really have any impact on the way I actually live my life. . . ." But is that really true?

A study conducted by University of Washington psychologists Elizabeth Loftus and John Palmer (as reported in *The Human Connection* by Martin Bolt and David Myers [Downers Grove, Ill.: InterVarsity Press, 1984]) shows just how powerfully we are influenced by what we hear and see. Loftus and Palmer showed two groups of people the same film of a traffic accident. Then one group was asked, "How fast were the cars going when they smashed into each other?" The other group was asked, "How fast were the cars going when they hit each other?"

Those in the first group, who were asked the question using the word *smashed*, gave consistently higher estimates of the impact speed than those in the second group, who were asked the same question using the word *hit*. In fact, even one week later, when the subjects were asked whether they recalled seeing any broken glass, researchers found the same effect. There was, in fact, no broken glass in the accident, but those who were asked the question using the word *smashed* were more than twice as likely to report broken glass than those who were asked the question using the word *hit*.

Now remember, these people had all seen the same accident with their own eyes! Their interpretation of events was significantly different just on the basis of one little word. What, might we suppose, is the impact of an entire song with lots of words and phrases that we hear over and over again? Or a two-hour movie with words and images combined?

So what can we do? We can learn to look deeper than appearances. We can begin to listen for half-truths: not just what the message is saying, but what it's not saying. What is being left out?

I live in suburban Philadelphia and I'm an avid fan of the Eagles. At one of our football games last season, there was so much crowd violence that officials considered stopping the contest. People were packing radio batteries inside snowballs and throwing them at spectators, referees, players, and any other convenient target. It was a nationally televised embarrassment for the City of Brotherly Love.

When the police and stadium authorities interviewed people after the game, 99 percent of those interviewed said the problems were due to the unrestricted sale of beer at the concession stands. These Sunday warriors came out, got tanked up, and started acting like idiots.

The irony of the whole sitaution is that the national telecast of the game was sponsored by several beer companies. There were beer banners all over the stadium and on the scoreboard. The subtle, unspoken message is that alcohol and sports go together, and that good sports fans are good drinkers. The reality of the situation was that all that good beer and all those good drinkers darn near killed each other, and almost caused the game to be canceled.

Consider Your Options. One of the most important skills to develop for making wise decisions is learning to think in terms of options and consequences. "There are three guys that might invite me to the dance next Friday. If I say no to Eric, what if Brian doesn't call? What if he does call and I have already said yes to Eric? What about the fact that I have already told Jason that I would go with him? Is it really likely that I will be able to talk Eric into going to the dance with Brian?" We can't make wise decisions without thinking through possible options and possible consequences.

This means, first of all, that we have to realize that there is more than one pathway to most destinations. If I want to travel to center-city Philly from my home near Valley Forge, there are several different routes I can take. Each of those routes has advantages and disadvantages. Some have better scenery, but more traffic; others have less traffic, but bad scenery; and then there's the Schuylkill Expressway that has bad scenery and bad traffic—but it's faster.

In making a careful decision, we need to play out

what consequences might result from each of the routes—each of the choices—available to us. Here's a strategy to help do that: Draw a diagram like the one below. If you're from basketball country, think of it is an NCAA tournament diagram. If you're from farm country, think of it as two back-to-back pitchforks. If you're Shirley MacLaine, think of it as your deceased uncle.

List options   **Best option**   **List consequences**

1 _____   _____ 1

2 _____   _____ 2

3 _____   _____ 3

To think through a decision, use the three lines (you can add more) on the left-hand side of the diagram to write down your options. Then, choose one of those options (you can choose another one later) and write it on the blank in the middle. Then, assuming that you have chosen to make the decision that you've listed in the middle blank, write down in the blanks on the right-hand side what three things are likely to result. That's stage one.

For extra credit, take each of the three results that you've written out in the blanks on the right, and go through the same process for each of them.

Try doing this right now. Pick some issue that you are dealing with and start with the three lines on the left. Remember: Choose your own adventure!

What this little game does is help you to think through options and consequences. Essentially, it helps you develop the habit of thinking through your choices more than one move ahead. You see, most of us don't do that; we respond on a reflex basis. "If it feels good, do it." We don't take time to ask ourselves the following kinds of questions:

- Will it still feel good one month or one year from now?
- What kinds of consequences might result from this feel good option that will not feel so good?
- What if I decide it does not feel good after I've made my decision—is there any way out?
- Will what makes me feel good make someone else feel bad?
- Are there other options open to me that might feel equally good, but not have the same negative consequences?
- Is feeling good my ultimate goal? Are there other values more important to me than feeling good that might make this a bad decision?

Seek the Will of God. As Christians, one of the ways we have to sift through the options and choices is by asking ourselves, "What is God's will in all of this?" What is it that God wants us to do? God makes his will known to us in many ways: sometimes through other Christians we respect, sometimes through an "inner voice" in our own spirit (our conscience), and sometimes he writes on our lawn with ice cubes in July (pay attention when this occurs!). But, the one absolutely trustworthy way of knowing his will is to read his Word.

In the Scripture, God gives us two different kinds of guidelines: precepts and principles. A *precept* is what we're given when we drive down an interstate highway and see a sign clearly stating, "Speed Limit 65." It is clear from this precept that there is a set limit for traffic on the interstate. That is the law.

119

Precepts are those signposts God puts in his Word that tell us what we are and what we are not to do. Precepts are those obvious statements God makes about various issues. "Do not lie. Do not steal. Do not commit adultery. Do not bear false witness. Do not covet." We don't have to pray about this stuff. When we pray about these issues, it's usually not because we're really seeking God's will, it's because we're trying to change God's will.

But what about the questions that fall between the cracks? Sure, the Bible says not to have sex before marriage; but what about all of the other sexual intimacy that is not excluded by that specific precept? That is where we are guided by *principles*. Where a specific speed is not posted, we might read a sign that says simply, "Drive Carefully." That's a principle.

As we read through the pages of Scripture, we see many situations in which God doesn't give us a specific law, but he gives us the guidelines of a basic principle. In other words, God doesn't tell us which play to run. He shows us the boundaries and the goal and says, "You make the call."

For example, although Paul does not give a specific law about which foods were "clean" or "unclean," he gives this basic principle: ". . . make up your mind not to put any stumbling block or obstacle in your brother's way. As one who is in the Lord Jesus, I am fully convinced that no food is unclean in itself. . . . Let us therefore make every effort to do what leads to peace and to mutual edification" (Romans 14:13-14, 19). That's a principle. It doesn't say, "Eateth this," or "Don't eateth that," it just gives us some guidelines.

The following are some verses that either explicitly state or imply some guidelines or principles. Why don't you get your Bible and see if you can identify some of them? (You know, your <u>Bible</u>—the big, black book with the funny gold lettering that's buried underneath your comic book collection.) Hebrews 12:1; 1 Corinthians 6:12; Romans 14:13; Colossians 4:5; 1 Corinthians 10:23; 1 Corinthians 10:31; 1 John 2:6; Leviticus 19:18; Matthew 18:21,22; Luke 12:37-48; Romans 12:2; Romans 12:10; Romans 12:18; Romans 13:1; Galatians 6:10; 1 Corinthians 6:19; 2 Corinthians 6:14.

Decide to Decide. I chuckled the other day as I watched a father chase his little boy through a department store. When the father finally caught up with his son, they were standing in front of me on the escalator. I overheard the boy ask his father if they could go upstairs to the toy section. The father, obviously not eager for this adventure in Nintendo-lust, said "I'll think about it." It was a great picture. The father had made no decision to go upstairs. He was "thinking about it." But with every passing moment the escalator was carrying him up to the threshold of toyland.

The final key for making wise decisons is simply deciding to decide. One of the main reasons that most of us make bad decisions is not that we have willfully, boldly decided to go out and sin. Sometimes that is the case. But not normally. I really don't believe most of the people reading this book are going to huddle together with a group of friends this Friday afternoon and say, "Hey, let's go out tonight and transgress the law of God. Y'wanna? We can break commandments three, seven, and nine. It'll be awesome!"

In most cases, we make a bad decision because we have made no decision at all. What usually happens is that you're at the Friday night basketball game and at halftime you see a whole flock of kids get up and walk out. You ask where they're going and they say to a movie. So, off you go, headed to the movies, or so you think. On the way to the movies, you meet a carload of people who are on their way to a party. And after a few minutes of conversation, everybody decides to head to the party.

Then, when you get to the party, you see some things you're not sure about. People are getting wasted on drugs and booze and slipping off into the bedrooms. But you feel funny walking out at that point, so you hang around. And of course, now the pressure builds and the resistance weakens. Before the night is over, you're making some decisions you had no intention of making—because you had decided nothing beforehand.

> *We can't make wise decisions if we make no decisions. It's always easier to balance a moving bicycle.*

We can't make wise decisions if we make no decisions. It's always easier to balance a bicycle that is moving. When we work through an issue, sometimes it's helpful to say, "I will go ahead and make this decision now. It will not keep me from other options later, but it does give me a direction in which to start moving." That may be what the Bible is talking about when it talks about a step of faith—it's that first decision to make a decision. Sometimes we wait to say yes or no and then our options have disappeared.

Guidance for the long haul

WHETHER WE'RE TALKING ABOUT GUIDANCE over the long haul, or specific prayer about a specific problem, the great news is that God wants us to make the right decision even more than we do. He loves us so much that he will always go out of his way to keep us on his way. That's the kind of God you want to have when you're working your way through the jungle.

> I will instruct you and teach you in the way you should go; I will counsel you and watch over you. Do not be like the horse or the mule, which have no understanding but must be controlled by bit and bridle or they will will not come to you. Many are the woes of the wicked, but the Lord's unfailing love surrounds the man who trusts in him. Rejoice in the Lord and be glad, you righteous; sing, all you who are upright in heart! *Psalm 32:8-11*

Chapter 10:
Breaking the tape

L ONGTIME VIEWERS (LIKE ME) of ABC TV's *Wide
World of Sports* still remember one of the most
dramatic moments in that show's thirty-year
broadcast history. It was during the 1973 Ironman and
Ironwoman Triathlon in Hawaii (a 148-mile swim-bike-
run event that challenges even the world's best triath-
letes), when twenty-three-year-old Julie Moss had a
dramatic finish.

The spectacle unfolded as Julie staggered her way
through the last several hundred feet of the race. It was
obvious almost immediately that she was in trouble.
The closer she got to the finish line, the clearer it was
that she was in pain. More stumbling than running,
Julie pushed herself all the way down to the last hundred or so steps until, all of a sudden, she just collapsed
about sixty feet from the finish line.

The crowd, hushed by the drama on the street in
front of them, watched with a mixture of fear and hope.
Some shouted words of encouragement. Others
gasped as she hit the hot pavement. For long moments,
the camera simply watched as Julie Moss heaved on
the pavement, gasping for air. Her hands inched forward, clawing at the asphalt.

Finally, after long, agonizing minutes, she once
again staggered to her feet, stumbled several more

steps . . . and then collapsed again in a heap, just a few feet from the finish line. The expression of pain on her face was unmistakable. The crowd could feel her agony. After a few moments, she mustered up the strength to stand again, only to stagger a few steps more before she fell one more time. It happened three times. Julie Moss would half-stand, stagger, stumble, and then collapse again on the pavement.

The last time she fell, it looked as if she might not rise again. Even the announcers didn't speak as viewers watched this drama, almost sensing that the only appropriate response in the face of such singular struggle was a kind of reverence. When Julie's trainer ran out to help her, she made one feeble gesture with her hand to flag him away, fearing that if he touched her in any way she would be disqualified from the race.

Finally, in a last incredible triumph of sheer guts and single-minded determination, twenty-three-year-old Julie Moss got to her feet, half-walked, half-crawled, and crossed the finish line to the thunderous cheers of the crowd. It was an incredible moment.

Ultimately, what really made the race remarkable that day was not the fact that the course was completed in record time, or even who finished first and emerged victorious. What really awed everyone that day was that one person was single-mindedly determined to go the distance, no matter what.

Staying power

MANY OF US HAVE BEEN THERE. It's the last night of camp, or Saturday night on a weekend retreat, and the speaker begins to make some sort of invitation: "If you're really serious about Jesus tonight, I'd like to invite you to come up here and stand with me next to this fire. . . . Or if you're *really* serious about Jesus tonight, I want to invite you to come up here and throw a piece of wood on the fire. . . . Or, if you're *really,* REALLY serious about Jesus, just come up here right now and stand *in* this fire!"

It's always exciting to see people come to Jesus. The Scripture says that multitudes in heaven rejoice over only "one sinner who re-pents." That's where new life begins! But, the key in the Christian life is not just *com-ing* to Jesus; it's developing *staying power* in Jesus, re-maining in him. The Chris-tian life is not about coming forward; it's about pressing onward. It's not a Carl Lewis 100-yard sprint; it's a Julie Moss triathlon.

Too often, we live our faith in short stretches. I call it "Tarzan Christianity," a Christiani-ty that only exists in the treetops. Tarzan was one of my comic book heroes when I was a little kid. He was the perfect picture of ma-cho, swinging through the jun-gle from vine to vine, calling to elephants, laughing with hyenas, and petting snakes. Dressed in this little leopard-skin number, with muscles on muscles, he was amazing! But one thing used to puzzle me about Tarzan when he took to the trees: How did it always happen that

> *God is always running alongside you, cheering and yelling, "Come on . . . let's break that tape!"*

there was a loose vine right there, right when he needed it, at just the right height for him to continue his jungle romp?

I used to lie awake some nights worrying about this: What happens when Tarzan comes to a clearing? I mean, here he is blitzing through the trees, a Mutant Ninja Jungle Boy, swinging from vine to vine, and, all of a sudden . . . a clearing. No trees! No vines! Just a screaming, yodeling blur of muscle and leopard skin flying through the air. "Tarzan Christians" swing from retreat to retreat, summer camp to summer camp, concert to concert. Every now and then they might dip down on their campus and kick a few of the "natives," but they spend most of their time swinging in the treetops and making a lot of noise, but not really accomplishing much.

The problem with "Tarzan Christianity" is that sooner or later, we're going to come to the clearing. We're going to run out of concerts or summer camps or conferences. It's just going to be us and Jesus, down there in the jungle—and that's when we really discover what our faith is made of.

For most of you who have read this book, your jungle has more lockers than leopards, more teachers than tigers, and it's not usually the elephant that is trumpeting to the herd.

In the triathlon race that most of us are running, there aren't many banners, there may not be that many cheers, and it probably won't be recorded on TV. But, we do have a Father in heaven who comes to all of our meets, and runs with us every step of the way. And as we learn to remain in him, day after day, he can give us the power to make it to the finish line and break the tape.

My deepest prayer, as you finish this book, is that

the world might see that same determination in me, and that it might see it in you, too. We may not be first, and we may not be fast, but we can be determined to *finish*.

And who knows? If you're quiet long enough when you close this book, you might even hear him cheering for you—because he is on your side. Don't forget that he's there when you're staggering through the toughest parts of your marathon, when it's "gut-check" time. This God who loves you is always running alongside you, cheering and yelling, "Come on . . . let's break that tape! . . . Press on. . . . Me and you. . . . We're going the distance!"